WILDSAM
FIELD GUIDES

Our list of gratitude stretches throughout the borough and
beyond. First, to the editorial contributors who helped bring the
Brooklyn soul to these pages — Tim Irwin, Sadie Stein, Brooke
Porter Katz, Wesley Verhoeve, Mikki Brammer, Sarah Gearhart,
Scott Ellman and Ben Barnes. Thank you! To our city editor,
Gina Hamadey, our genuine appreciation for your Brooklyn
smarts and dedication. A special thank you to the Brooklyn
Historical Society and their archival staff; The Brooklyn Public
Library; Tom Hinkel and Laura Shunk at the Village Voice;
Nick Fauchald and Kaitlyn Goalen at Short Stack Editions; and
Halimah Marcus at Electric Literature. To Lauren Tamaki, you
are a joy and your illustrations are fabulous. To Emma Straub
and Marie-Helene Bertino, thank you for sharing such beautiful
essays. And to our Bk friends — Bruce and Katherine Crane,
Christie Chow, Ben Fuqua, Marc Menchaca, Reid Rolls,
Emily Grant, Benjamin Samuel, Weldon Pless, Cory Cavin,
Caroline Taylor — you're Brooklyn's best.

WILDSAM FIELD GUIDES™

ISBN 978-1-4951-1286-7

Art direction by Stitch Design Co.
Illustrations by Lauren Tamaki

www.wildsam.com

⠀⠀≫ CONTENTS ≪

⟫ WELCOME ⟪

HERE'S A MEMORY. On an October afternoon in 2009, I received a call from a loose acquaintance, asking if I'd be available to help pack up an apartment later that night. It was a fourth-floor walkup in Brooklyn Heights, and there would be beer. "Clara from Brooklyn College thought you'd be interested," the caller said. "It's Norman Mailer's place."

I remember the clear sky that evening. I remember noticing that, even though he'd died two years before, the apartment looked as if Mailer had just stepped out to buy bread. Newspaper folded on the table. Coffee beans in the cupboard. I remember six or seven lamps glowing, books crammed everywhere, and I remember that the balcony door was wide-open and that a calm breeze blew in as the BQE hummed below. I remember holding Mailer's copy of *The Naked and the Dead*, and seeing his evening view, across the river, of the giant glass city lit-up from within. And I remember wondering, What happens to you if this is where you live and this is what you see every day?

This is Brooklyn. Even for the deeper neighborhoods—Crown Heights, Bedford-Stuyvesant, Bensonhurst, Canarsie, Mill Basin— Brooklyn begins with its proximity. It wrestles with what James Agee called the "mad magnetic energy" that burns non-stop across the river. For hundreds of years, the tension between that place and this one, of what is and what can be, has been where Brooklyn thrives. For the no-name screenwriter and the playground baller, for the man who'd be mayor and the woman who'd sit on the Supreme Court, for the Italian restaurateur and the Haitian cab driver, for them and thousands of others, Brooklyn is the proving ground. It is the most fertile soil for American narratives—the stranger in a strange land, the underdog, the self-made.

Mel Brooks and Mos Def, Barbra Streisand and Lena Horne, Sandy Koufax and Spike Lee. And the three hundred and eighty years of immigrant families, whose immeasurable risk and hustle and ambition is the American mystique. It came from these seventy-one square miles across the East River. It came from Brooklyn. *-TB*

ESSENTIALS

NAVIGATION

CITY APP
Hopstop
NYC Wifi + Coffee

....

RIVER FERRY
Dumbo
Old Fulton Street

Shaefer Landing
440 Kent Ave

....

BICYCLES
Ride Brooklyn
Park Slope, Williamsburg
ridebrooklynny.com

HOTELS

DESIGN
Wythe Hotel
80 Wythe Ave
wythehotel.com

....

BED AND BREAKFAST
Urban Cowboy
111 Powers St
urbancowboybnb.com

....

APARTMENTS
oneandonly.com
airbnb.com

COFFEE

GREENPOINT
Budin
114 Greenpoint Ave

WILLIAMSBURG
Devocion
69 Grand St

....

COBBLE HILL
Café Pedlar
210 Court St

....

CARROLL GARDENS
Smith Canteen
343 Smith St

....

PROSPECT HTS
Hungry Ghost
253 Flatbush Ave

CALENDAR
JAN   Coney Island Polar Bear Club
FEB   Chinese New Years
MAR   CasHank Hootenanny
APR   Cherry Blossom Festival
MAY   Five Borough Bike Tour
JUN   Bushwick Open Studios
JUL   Hip-Hop Festival
AUG   West Indian Carnival
SEP   Brooklyn Book Festival
OCT   Pumpkin Carving Contest
NOV   BAM Next Wave Festival
DEC   Dyker Heights Lights

BOOKS
☞ *Brooklyn Is* by James Agee
☞ *The Great Bridge*
   by David McCullough
☞ *A Fortress of Solitude*
   by Jonathan Lethem

ITINERARY

ONE DAY

Linger in Prospect Park
Steaks at Peter Luger
Maison Premiere nightcap

....

WEEKEND

Brunch at Marlow and Sons
Summer Rooftop Films series
Wander Brooklyn Flea
Visit Court Street Books
Dinner at Frankies Sputino
Walk Brooklyn Bridge Park

FOODWAY

Coal-Oven Pizza
At a scorching 1,200 degrees,
bulky coal-ovens bring out
Brooklyn's famous crusty char.

RADIO

Funkmaster Flex, Hot 97.1
The Leonard Lopate Show, 93.9
The Bowery Boys podcast

RECORD COLLECTION

Beastie Boys ....*Paul's Boutique*
Jay-Z.. *The Blueprint*
TV on the Radio .... *Dear Science*
Buddy Rich...*Rich Versus Roach*
Sharon Jones and the Dap-Kings ....*Learned the Hard Way*
Grizzly Bear .... *Yellow House*
Notorious B.I.G. ....*Ready to Die*
Big Daddy Kane..*Long Live the Kane*
The National ....*Boxer*
MC Lyte..*Lyte as a Rock*
The Lone Bellow..*The Lone Bellow*
Richie Havens...*Mixed Bag*
Mos Def & Talib Kweli ....*Black Star*

ESSENTIALS

PROGRESS

- Greenpoint credited as a national hub of rooftop agri culture advancements.
- From early 2012 to late 2013, controversial stop-and-frisk encounters in Brooklyn's Precinct 77 have gone from 100 per day to relatively few.
- Since 1990, Brooklyn's crime has decreased by 77%.
- By 2015, Brooklyn tech firms are projected to contribute over $6 billion to the local economy.
- In 2012, the Freelancer's Union opened the nation's first clinic specifically for the independent workforce.
- At nationally-renowned Brooklyn Tech High, over 72% of students qualify as economically disadvantaged.
- Over 37% residents are foreign born, three times the national average.
- In 2014, Brooklyn-based Etsy had 54 million registered members.

POTENTIAL

- Average weekly wage in Brooklyn is $760 compared to $2,749 in Manhattan.
- Since 2014, price per square foot in Williamsburg has increased by 174%.
- According to EPA, the Gowanus Canal is one of nation's most contaminated bodies of water.
- Park Slope senior citizens group continue 2011 lawsuit to remove bike lane near Prospect Park.
- A quarter of Brooklyn residents receive food stamps, compared to national average of 15%.
- The Brooklyn high school graduation rate of 42.7% falls behind both broader city and state.
- Median income in Brownsville is $26,273. Park Slope's is $88,610.
- In 2014, the NBA's Knicks accrued $66 million more in revenue than Brooklyn'sNets.

STATISTICS

82,686	People who are self-employed
136	Languages spoken in Brooklyn
419	Homicides in 2014 [lowest number in 50 years]
10,267	Number of apartment buildings
983,160	Tons of garbage collected annually
41	Average commute time to work in minutes

BROOKLYN NEIGHBORHODS ➡

BROOKLYN NEIGHBORHODS ➡

🛣 495

🛣 78

○ GREENPOINT

○ WILLIAMSBURG

○ DUMBO   🛣 278

BROOKLYN HTS ○
FORT GREENE ○   BUSHWICK ○

COBBLE HILL ○
○ BOERUM HILL   ○ BED-STUY

○ CARROLL GARDENS

RED HOOK ○
○ PROSPECT HTS

GOWANUS ○
○ CROWN HTS

PARK SLOPE ○   BROWNSVILLE ○

PROSPECT-LEFFERTS GARDENS ○   EAST NEW YORK ☞

○ EAST FLATBUSH

DITMAS PARK ○   CANARSIE ○

○ BOROUGH PARK

○ BAY RIDGE   FLATLANDS ○

🛣 278 ○ DYKER HTS
MIDWOOD ○   BERGEN BEACH ○
○ BENSONHURST

MILL BASIN ○

GRAVESEND ○   ○ SHEEPSHEAD BAY

MANHATTAN BEACH ○
CONEY ISLAND ○   ○ BRIGHTON BEACH

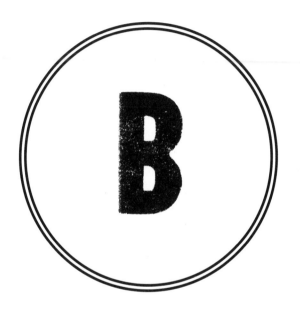

BESTS

A curated list of citywide favorites including corner cafes, pizza dens, beer bars, vinyl sellers, motorcycle shops, movie theaters, late night dancing and more.

⫸ FOOD & DRINK ⫷

*Note: See our "New Institutions" restaurant map
on page 52 for more favorites.*

NEIGHBORHOOD CAFÉ

Rucola

*190 Dean St
Boerum Hill
rucolabrooklyn.com*

Barnwood ceiling
echoes the farm-
focus menu.

·····················

CARIBBEAN

Gladys

*788 Franklin Ave
Crown Heights
gladysnyc.com*

Fresh Caribbean
joint serving jerk
chicken and spiked
slushies.

·····················

BRUNCH

Farm on Adderley

*1108 Cortelyou Road
Ditmas Park
thefarmonadderley.com*

Omelets and choco-
late bread in an
outdoor garden.

INSTITUTION

Peter Luger

*178 Broadway
Williamsburg
peterluger.com*

Time-travel to old
Bk, then hobnob
with a martini and
porterhouse.

·····················

CHINESE TAKEOUT

Lucky Eight

*5204 8th Ave
Sunset Park
lucky8cuisine.com*

Order the Pride
of Lucky Eight.

·····················

OYSTERS

Maison Premiere

*298 Bedford Ave
Williamsburg
maisonpremiere.com*

Half-shell it at
the marble U-bar
and partake in the
absinthe drip.

CHEF'S TABLE

Brooklyn Fare

*431 West 37th St
Boerum Hill
brooklynfare.com*

Three Michelin
stars, eighteen
seats, 100% worth
the hype.

·····················

MIDDLE EASTERN

Tanoreen

*7523 3rd Ave
Bay Ridge
tanoreen.com*

Mop plates of spiced
lamb or chicken fetti
with flat bread.

·····················

IRISH PUB

Kitty Kiernans

*9715 3rd Ave
Bay Ridge
kittykiernans.com*

Proper Guinness
pours and always full
of good craic.

PIZZA

Totonno's

1524 Neptune Ave
Coney Island
totonnosconeyisland.com

Never-ending
debate in NYC, this
pie palace has been
legit since 1924.

....

VIETNAMESE

Nightingale 9

329 Smith St
Carroll Gardens
nightingale9.com

Spiffy noodle shop
with Southern
roots, the soy ages
in bourbon barrels.

....

SPANISH

La Vara

268 Clinton St
Cobble Hill
lavarany.com

Tortas, croquetas
and paella fideuá on
picturesque brown-
stone block.

....

SATURDAY MORNING

Marlow & Sons

81 Broadway
Williamsburg
marlowandsons.com

A two-top by the
open window, one
egg-cheese biscuit
and a *Diner Journal*.

SOUL FOOD

Mitchell's

617A Vanderbilt Ave
Prospect Heights
[718] 789-3211

Fix your fried chick-
en and cornbread
cravings without
leaving Brooklyn.

....

UKRAINIAN

Café Glechik

3159 Coney Island Ave
Brighton Beach
glechik.com

Coney Island
Saturdays with the
famous dumplings
and borscht.

....

SANDWICHES

Mamma Louisa's Hero Shoppe

609 New York Ave
Prospect-Lefferts
Garden
718-773-7785

Smoked meats,
fresh challah rolls,
good beers. And
cheap. Our heroes.

....

DONUTS

Dough

448 Lafayette Ave
Bed-Stuy
doughbrooklyn.com

A little trendy, but
a lot delicious.

COCKTAILS

Long Island Bar

110 Atlantic Ave
Brooklyn Heights
thelongislandbar.com

Same old neon
marquee, fancy new
concoctions. And
best ice in Bk.

....

BEER

Torst

615 Manhattan Ave
Greenpoint
torstnyc.com

Minimal but cool
Danish brewers
room rotating
21 taps.

....

HANGOUT

Lavender Lake

383 Carroll St
Gowanus
lavenderlake.com

Grab your usual
order inside, chill
under twinklies
outside, repeat.

....

AL FRESCO

Hot Bird

825 Atlantic Ave
Prospect Heights

Revamped auto
shop turned bar
with a killer outdoor
space—especially
after snow melts.

⫸ SHOPPING ⫷

ANTIQUES
Holler & Squall
119 Atlantic Ave
Brooklyn Heights
hollerandsquall.com
Industrial and mid-century collection guarded by a herd of taxidermy.
....

FURNITURE
Strawser and Smith
487 Driggs Ave
Williamsburg
strawserandsmith.com
Lacquered benches, oak tables or a Hans Wegner rocker.
....

TERRARIUMS
Twig
287 3rd Ave
Gowanus
twigterrariums.com
Tiny eco-worlds of flora and rock, assembled or DIY.

RECORDS
Permanent Records
159 20th St
Greenpoint
permanentrecords.info
Spin everything from Dylan to D'Angelo, don't bypass the $1 bin.
....

FOUND OBJECTS
Brooklyn Flea
176 Lafayette Ave
Fort Greene
brooklynflea.com
Neighborhood bazaar, originators of Bk artisanal bent.
....

DENIM
Brooklyn Denim Co.
85 N 3rd St
Williamsburg
brooklyndenimco.com
Purveyor of classic and small-batch indigo.

MEN'S STYLE
Modern Anthology
68 Jay St
Dumbo
modernanthology.com
Home goods and clothing for gents who love vintage globes and raw denim.
....

WOMEN'S BOUTIQUE
Bird
316 Fifth Ave
Park Slope
shopbird.com
Brooklyn-chic, voted best woman's boutique by *New York*.
....

NECKTIES
Hickoree's Floor Two
109 6th St
Williamsburg
hickorees.com
Skinny-up with Hungarian camouflage and chambray.

JEWELRY

Catbird
219 Bedford Ave
Williamsburg
catbirdnyc.com
Basically invented the stack, wedding annex recently opened.

....

EYEGLASSES

Moscot
159 Court St
Cobble Hill
moscot.com
Fifth-generation purveyors of shades and hard-to-find frames.

....

BICYCLES

Redbeard Bikes
69 Jay St
Dumbo
redbeardbikes.com
Single-speeds for the urban commuter or a Liv Avail 3 for the long ride.

....

TOYS

Acorn
323 Atlantic Ave
Boerum Hill
acorntoyshop.com
Heirloom toysellers since 2004, cheek-squeezed by *Vogue* and *NYT*.

KID'S CURIO

Brooklyn Superhero Supply Co.
372 5th Ave
Park Slope
superherosupplies.com
Johnny needs a photon shooter and a can of cloning fluid.

....

ART BOOKS

Spoonbill and Sugartown
218 Bedford Ave
Williamsburg
spoonbillbooks.com
Thick stacks for the eclectically sophisticated thumber.

....

SURF

Pilgrim Surf Supply
68 N 3rd St
Williamsburg
pilgrimsurfsupply.com
Noseriders, longboards and westsuits for the weekend wave in Rockaway.

....

ARTISTS' SUPPLY

Artist & Craftman Supply
307 2nd St
Park Slope
artistcraftsman.com
One-stop shop for looms, yarns or filbert paintbrushes.

GOURMET GROCER

Foragers
56 Adams St
Dumbo
foragersmarket.com
Their upstate farm supplies fresh produce and heritage eggs.

....

WINE

Smith and Vine
268 Smith St
Carroll Gardens
smithandvine.com,
Vino for the under $10-cab crowd or the sophisticated somm.

....

BUTCHER

The Meat Hook
100 Frost St
Williamsburg
the-meathook.com
Housemade cold cuts, dry-aged NY beef and thick bacon dreams — right off the BQE.

....

CHEESE

Stinky Bklyn
215 Smith St
Cobble Hill
stinkybklyn.com
Cheesemongers encourage their samplers to linger.

≫ ACTION ≪

MOVIE THEATER

Nitehawk Cinema
136 Metropolitan Ave
Williamsburg
nitehawkcinema.com
Signature Series
pairs cocktails and
food around a movie.
....

LIVE MUSIC

CasHank Hoote-
nanny Jamboree
Freddy's Bar
627 5th Ave
Country jam ses-
sions with a strict
four-chord rule.
....

CULTURE

BAM
Fort Greene
bam.org
*A Streetcar Named
Desire,* the Nation-
al, Brazilian dance
groups—and that's
just last week.

MUSEUM

Brooklyn Museum
200 Eastern Parkway
Crown Heights
brooklynmuseum.org
Collection of 1.5
million works,
including a center
for feminist art.
....

COOKING CLASS

The Brooklyn
Kitchen
100 Frost St
Williamsburg
thebrooklynkitchen.com
Snout-to-tail pig
butchering, dump-
ling wrapping.
....

DANCING

Friends & Lovers
641 Classon Ave
Crown Heights
Old-school hip-hop
dance parties until
4am kind of place.

PICK-UP BALL

Pier 2
150 Furman St
Brooklyn Heights
Lace 'em up tight,
we hear this is the
borough's best spot
to run full-court.
....

PARADE

West Indian Parade
325 Rogers Ave
Crown Heights
wiadcacarnival.org
Pan-Caribbean festi-
val of masqueraders
and rowdy steel
bands competition.
....

BOWLING

Melody Lanes
461 37th St
Sunset Park
melodylanesny.com
Retro alley with
beloved barman
Pete Napolitano.

VIEW

Promenade
*Montague St &
Pierrepont Pl
Brooklyn Heights*
A soaring, shimmery vista that stoked Whitman, Mailer and millions more dreamers.
....

HISTORY

Fidler-Wyckoff House
*5816 Clarendon Rd
East Flatbush
wyckoffmuseum.org*
Built in 1652 by Dutch immigrants, oldest house in NYC.
....

WEIRD

Morbid Anatomy Museum
*424-A 3rd Ave
Gowanus*
Home to bizarre and the macabre — four-eyed kitties, a scrapbook of hair. The usual.
....

SHUFFLEBOARD

Royal Palms
*514 Union St
Gowanus
royalpalmsshuffle.com*
Kickstarted courts rent by the hour.

SHAKESPEARE

Theatre for a New Audience
*162 Ashland Place
Downtown
tfana.org*
Contemporary takes on the Bard in an Elizabethan courtyard.
....

COMEDY SHOW

Big Terrific
*Cameo Gallery
93 N 6th St
Williamsburg*
Free, weekly stand-up every Wednesday, follow @silvestri for the lineup.
....

SWIMMING POOL

McCarren Park
*776 Lorimer St
Williamsburg
mccarrenpark.com*
Cool off with the summer crowds after wandering 35 acres of trails.
....

PICNIC

Prospect Park
prospectpark.org
Six hundred rolling acres to make you forget about that other park across the river.

CHURCH SERVICE

Brooklyn Tabernacle Choir
*17 Smith St
Downtown*
Snag a pew and settle in for booming gospel from the six-time Grammy winners.
....

SUMMER NIGHTS

Rooftop Films
rooftopfilms.com
Indie film screenings all over borough, two thumbs up for Industry City venue.
....

SLEDDING

Fort Greene Park
*Myrtle Ave
Fort Greene
fortgreenepark.org*
Four hills of snowy fun, with greased trashcan lids, daredevils go for the Triple Steps.
....

BOCCE

Union Hall
*702 Union St
Park Slope
unionhallny.com*
Velvet sofas and lanes upstairs, music venue downstairs.

≫ EXPERTISE ≪

RARE GUITARS

Retrofret Guitars
233 Butler St
Gowanus
retrofret.com
Pick around for a
1932 Gibson L-4 or
maybe a Snakehead
mandolin.

....

PIANO MOVING

Bill Rogers
thepianomover.com
Carefully hoisting
Baby Grands from
fourth-floor walkups
and barely tickling
the ivories.

....

FASHION STYLING

Kelly Framel
theglamourai.com
Dolce & Gabbana
and Ralph Lauren,
editor of esteemed
fashion blog, The
Glamourai.

TATTOOS

Flyrite
492 Metropolitan Ave
Williamsburg
flyritetattoo.nyc
Parlor admired for
cleanest of lines.
Mike is the guy for
script.

....

FILM EDITING

T.J. Misny
tjmisny.com
Her documen-
tary, Scattered, won
"Best Editing" at
2012 Brooklyn Film
Festival.

....

FLORAL DESIGN

Ingrid Carozzi
tincanstudiosbk.com
Bridal bouquets
with antique French
ribbons, rustic
arrangements in
reclaimed vessels.

RUNNING

Brooklyn Road
Runners
Park Slope
brooklynroadrun-
ners.org
Group runs meet
four times per week
in Prospect Park.

....

CHESS

Danny Kopec
kopecchess.com
Lecturer on chess
history and strate-
gies, second place
finisher at the
U.S. Open.

....

POLLUTION

Brooklyn Atlantis
brooklynatlantis.
poly.edu
Collection of
scientists launched
a robot to clean up
the Gowanus Canal.

LETTERPRESS

The Arm
281 N 7th St
Williamsburg
thearmnyc.com

Reserve solo time on a giant Vandercook or ink-up your fingers in workshops.

....

BED BUGS

Bed Bug Inspection Group
215 S 4th St
Williamsburg
bedbuginspection-group.com

Jon and his sniffer-beagle Daisy are pros — though we hope you don't need them.

....

MOTORCYCLE RESTORATION

Moto Borgotaro
97 Union St
Columbia Waterfront
motoborgotaro.com

Tune-ups and custom rebuilds — Ducati, Triumph, BMW, Laverdas. Start saving up.

....

RESTAURATEUR

Andrew Tarlow
marlowandsons.com

Diner, Reynard and Marlow's wonderful Williamsburg duo.

FICTION WRITING

Joshua Henkin
joshuahenkin.com

Award-winning novelist coordinates rigorous, popular Brooklyn College M.F.A. program.

....

DANCE INSTRUCTION

Cynthia King Dance
1256 Prospect Ave
Windsor Terrace
cynthiakingdance.com

Choreography and dance ed classes ranging from classical to emerging style.

....

HAND LETTERING

Dana Tanamachi
Crown Heights
tanamachistudio.com
@danatanamachi

Large-scale chalk and patterned typography for brands like Target, Nike, *Time* Magazine and Oprah.

....

BROWNSTONE RENOVATION

MADE
made-nyc.com

Designers and contractors share one roof in this non-traditional and smart firm.

TAILOR

Fulani
496 Flatbush Ave
Prospect-Lefferts
Gardens

Tapering, alterations, and suiting fixes for every level of dandy.

....

LOCKSMITH

M&D Locksmith
1004 Cortelyou Rd
Ditmas Park
brooklynmanhattan-locksmith.com

Trustworthy, speedy and professional. Ask for Joey.

....

LIGHTING DESIGN

Workstead
232 3rd St E102
Gowanus
workstead.com

Minimalist chandeliers and lamps, bent steel sophistication seen in Wythe Hotel.

....

DOG GROOMING

Sonia's Pet Grooming
471 Seventh Ave
Park Slope
soniaspetgrooming.com

Happy yelps from all the neighborhood pups.

ALMANAC

A deep dive into the cultural heritage of Brooklyn through timelines, newspaper clippings, how-to's, personal notes and other written forms of nostalgia.

BROOKLYN DODGERS

> *In the late 1800s, Brooklyn dubbed its baseball club the "Trolley Dodgers," a nod to the newly electric, often dangerous trolley cars. By the 1940s, the team was simply the Dodgers, playing their home games at Ebbets Field in Flatbush and breaking the baseball color line in 1946 with Jackie Robinson. Ten years later, owner Walter O'Malley decided to uproot for sunny Los Angeles. When borough president John Cashmore heard the rumor, he sent this telegram.*

SEPT 8 1957

DEAR WALTER

REPORTS HERE INDICATE LOS ANGELES REPRESENTATIVE HAS CONFERRED WITH YOU THIS MORNING IN EARNEST SUGGESTION IS THAT YOU WITHHOLD FINAL COMMITMENT WITH THEM I AM STRIVING TO ARRIVE AT SOLUTION OF THE PROBLEM HERE AS YOU KNOW REPORT IS PENDING ON LEGALITY OF MAKING LAND AVAILABLE FOR DODGER STADIUM IT IS EXPECTED MOMENTARILY. AS I TOLD YOU I AM DOING EVERYTHING POSSIBLE TO SEE THAT THE BEST INTEREST OF THE CITY THE TAXPAYERS AND BROOKLYN DODGERS-- AND ESPECIALLY THE PROPERTY OWNERS IN THE AREA INVOLVED ARE SAFEGUARDED. OVER AND ABOVE THIS, WALTER, ALL OF US HAVE A RESPONSIBILITY TO THE MILLIONS OF DODGER FANS WHO HAVE SUPPORTED THE DODGERS AND WANT TO SEE THEM REMAIN IN IN BROOKLYN. MOREOVER, ALL OF US ARE AGREED THAT AS A SYMBOL TO YOUTH AND TO THE WORLD OF SPORTS, THE DODGERS AND BROOKLYN ARE AN IMMORTAL COMBINATION. BASEBALL WILL NOT BE BASEBALL WITHOUT THE DODGERS IN BROOKLYN. AND I DON,T THINK I WOULD BE ABLE TO EVER AGAIN FACE A YOUNGSTER IN BROOKLYN OR ANYWHERE, IF I DIDNT DO EVERYTHING I COULD WITHIN REASON TO KEEP THE DODGERS IN BROOKLYN. PLEASE HOLD EVERYTHING--- AND TELL THE LOS ANGELES TO GO FIND ITSELF ANOTHER BASEBALL TEAM

SINCERELY

JOHN CASHMORE PRESIDENT BOROUGH OF BROOKLYN

MOBSTERS OF NOTE

Life	Nickname	Infamy
1897-1944	Lepke	Louis Buchalter, first boss to receive death penalty
1897-1962	Lucky	Charles Luciano ran Commission crime network, was granted secret WWII prison deal by gov't
1899-1947	Scarface	Al Capone grew up in Park Slope, face slashed while working at Brooklyn nightclub
1902-1957	The Mad Hatter	Albert Anastasia led Murder Inc. and Gambinos ruthlessly
1905-2002	Joe Bananas	After Castellammarese War, Joseph Bonanno become youngest of crime family bosses
1906-1947	Bugsy	Famously handsome, Benjamin Siegel became mob celebrity and Vegas financier
1906-1941	Kid Twist	Informant Abe Reles "fell" to death from Coney Island balcony
1906-1976	Tick-Tock	Jewish hitman Albert Tannenbaum was a trusted solder for Lepke Buchalter
1910-1979	The Cigar	Carmine Galante, shot to death in Bushwick restaurant, cigar still in mouth
1915-1985	Big Paulie	Butcher's son Paul Castellano inherited Gambinos until John Gotti put hit out
1930-1981	Sonny Black	Williamsburg local, Dominic Napolitano, let FBI agent "Donnie Brasco" infiltrate gang
1931-1996	Jimmy the Gent	James Burke planned JFK airport heist, master at bribing cops for witness names

THE BROOKLYN BRIDGE

1841	German immigrant John Roebling produces wire rope in Pennsylvania.
1846	Roebling completes his first suspension bridge in Pittsburgh.
1855	Roebling completes a suspension bridge in Niagara Falls.
1865	Roebling's son, Washington, returns from Civil War, notably manning hot air balloon to scout enemy before Battle of Gettysburg.
1867	Roebling appointed chief engineer of the Brooklyn Bridge.
1869	Standing on pilings, Roebling slips, foot is crushed, and gangrene sets in. Dies two weeks later. Last words are "The bridge will be beautiful!" Trustees appoint Washington Roebling, 32, chief engineer.
1870	Construction begins by sinking two pneumatic, 3000-ton caissons deep into the riverbed.
1871	Brooklyn caisson finally reaches bedrock, tons of concrete poured into empty chambers.
1872	Men working inside second caisson suffer from the bends. Roebling crippled by the disease, bedridden in Brooklyn Heights.
1873	Boss Tweed, bridge trustee, convicted of stealing funds
1876	First steel rope strung across towers.
1878	Cables finished, steel suspenders hung from cables.
1883	At 1,595 feet, the Brooklyn Bridge is completed. Roebling's wife, Emily, crosses first in a carriage.
	May 24, opens to public, 250,000 people cross the next day.
	Memorial Day, panic over a rumor of collapse. Twelve people are crushed to death.
	Toll is a penny for pedestrians, five cents for a horse.
1884	P.T. Barnum takes 21 elephants over bridge to prove safety.
1885	Robert Odlum, a swimming instructor from Washington, D.C., dies from bridge leap.

THE ELEPHANTS CROSS THE BRIDGE

New York Times
May 18, 1884

England's pet, old Jumbo, his Royal Sacredness, the white elephant, and the mighty name of Barnum added a new lustre to the bridge last night. To people who looked up from the river at the big arch of electric lights it seemed as if Noah's ark were emptying itself over on Long Island. At 9:30 o'clock 21 elephants, 7 camels, and 10 dromedaries issued from the ferry at the foot of Courtland-street. "Hooray!" shouted a small boy, "there's Jumbo!" His signal spread like a financial crisis, and soon all his tribe were leading, lining, and following the procession up Broadway to the bridge. At the order of the Superintendent of Tolls no fare was collected. The bridge rules fix the fares for man, neat cattle, and horses. The question of how much an elephant or a dromedary should pay stumped the Superintendent, and until he has solved the problem Barnum will enjoy the use of his money. The white elephant, mindful of his sacred character, followed with dignity. The other elephants shuffled along, raising their trunks and snorting as every train went by. Old Jumbo brought up the rear. As he reached Brooklyn he waved his ears in acknowledgement of a prolonged chorus of delighted "ons!" from a whole house-top full of pretty girls. In the City of Churches the procession filed through a tremendous crowd to the show grounds, at Tompkins and Fulton avenues. The wagons and the rest of the animals, under the charge of R.D. Hamilton, were transferred by the Annex and Fulton ferry. A big parade will be given on Monday morning, and the first performance will be in the afternoon.

DOMINO SUGAR

"Explosion Wrecks Big Sugar Plant"
The New York Times
June 14, 1917

FIFTEEN MEN TAKEN TO HOSPITALS, ONE DEAD, FOUR DYING—MANY STILL IN RUINS.

....

PRODUCT WAS FOR ALLIES

....

HINTS OF PLOT—FIREBOATS, ALL BROOKLYN ENGINES AND A DOZEN MORE AT WORK.

Twenty men—perhaps fifty—were buried in the debris of an eleven-story building of the American Sugar Refining Company's plant in Greenpoint, Brooklyn, last night when an explosion wrecked it.

At 1 o'clock this morning fifteen injured, one of whom died and four of whom are dying, had been taken out of the burning structure, and Fire Marshal Brophy said that at least a score of the 300 men who were at work in the building had not come out. At that time fire was raging, so that it was impossible to go into the place. Men who worked there were confident 100 men had been trapped in the building. At various hospitals between sixty and seventy men were treated for burns and other injuries.

The company has large orders for sugar for our allies and the particular building in which the explosion occurred was the structure from which refined sugar was loaded for export to Europe. Fire Marshal Brophy has started an investigation of suspicious circumstances surrounding the explosion. One guess hazarded as to its cause early this morning was that an electric spark might have caused the explosion.

Chief Kenlon said at 2:30 o'clock that the fire was under control. "How many are caught in that building there is no telling until we search it," he said, "and that can't be done for some hours yet."

The building at that time was a tottering wreck. One side had fallen in and the walls left standing were staggering so that dynamiting them was considered by the firemen. The windows for blocks in every direction had been shattered by the force of the explosion.

Lieutenant Flinn at the Lee Avenue Police Station was just receiving the report of 100 Home Defense Guards when he heard the explosion. He held them, located the fire, and sent them to the scene, where they did good work holding back the crowds, in which were the wives and children of many men working in the building, as well as the relatives of 2,000 men who worked in other parts of the plant. The police got the service of 100 Naval Reserves to help handle the crowds.

The engineer at the plant said he believed the explosion had been caused through the combustion of "sugar dust" by a spark from some source. The building was used partly as a warehouse, and the loss was estimated at $1,000,000.

With searchlights from boats in the harbor playing on the fire, which endangered the ten blocks of buildings of the great sugar plant, every piece of fire apparatus in Brooklyn, half a score of companies from Manhattan, and all the fireboats were pouring streams into the burning building at 1:30 o'clock to keep the flames from spreading.

The American Sugar Refining Company's plant in Williamsburg is its largest. It stretches from South Second Street along Kent Avenue to Grand Street. At Third Street and Kent Avenue stood an eleven-story structure for the making of a granulated sugar. It was in this building that the explosion occurred. A mixer reaches from the ground floor to the fifth floor. Just before midnight there was an explosion in this mixer which demolished the fifth, sixth, seventh, eighth, ninth, tenth, and eleventh stories, and took the roof off the structure.

The 300 men at work on the night shift scurried to the fire escapes and across a bridge which led to the top floor of a seven-story structure across Kent Avenue. Most of those who got out went by this latter route. The debris from the explosion feel back upon the building, wrecking all but its walls, and a fiercely burning fire started in the highly inflammable sugar.

MOVIES

FILM	NEIGHBORHOOD	YEAR
A Tree Grows in Brooklyn	Williamsburg	1945
The French Connection	Bensonhurst	1971
Dog Day Afternoon	Gravesend	1975
Saturday Night Fever	Bay Ridge	1977
The Warriors	Coney Island	1979
Sophie's Choice	Midwood	1982
Once Upon a Time in America	Dumbo	1984
Moonstruck	Brooklyn Heights	1987
Do The Right Thing	Bedford-Stuyvesant	1989
Goodfellas	East New York	1990
He Got Game	Coney Island	1998
Requiem For A Dream	Brighton Beach	2000
The Squid and the Whale	Park Slope	2005
Half Nelson	Gowanus	2006

NATHAN'S FAMOUS HOT DOGS

Nathan Handwerker opened Nathan's in Coney Island in 1916, charging a nickel per dog, half the price of his competitor. Through the twentieth century, Nathan's developed a famous fan base: President Franklin D. Roosevelt served the dogs to the king and queen of England, and had some sent to Yalta for his meeting with Churchill and Stalin. Barbra Streisand had the hot dogs shipped to London for a party, and Jacqueline Kennedy served them at the White House. In recent years the stand has gained fame for its annual hot dog eating contest. [Joey Chestnut holds the world record: 69 hot dogs in 10 minutes.] Nathan's still stands on the corner of Surf and Stillwell Avenues, open 365 days a year and closing just once, after Hurricane Sandy on October 29, 2012. After seven months and millions of dollars, Nathan's reopened with a hot dog link-cutting ceremony.

MAST BROTHERS CHOCOLATE

Brothers Michael and Rick Mast very much signify the Brooklyn of this new century. Artisanal. Design-savvy. Fearlessly DIY. From early days grinding down cacao in their apartment to their expanding operations in a renovated 1880s spice factory in Williamsburg, the Mast future is bright — and wrapped in exquisitely designed papers.

1. Source complex cacao from a global network of small farms.

2. Farmers in "cacao belt"—20 degrees north and south of equator—harvest mature pods.

3. Brightly colored pods resemble a football, hold 30-40 beans in citrusy membrane.

4. Farmers remove beans from pods for wild fermentation.

5. Three to six days fermenting brings out chocolaty qualities.

6. Beans then sun-dried on cement platforms or mesh tables, raked and stirred.

7. Select beans placed in 150-pound jute or burlap bags, imported to Brooklyn.

8. Mast team hand sorts beans over metal grid to remove twigs, rocks or split beans.

9. Lightly roast beans on low temp. Less time than you'd think.

10. Use winnower to separate papery husks from heavier nibs. Send leftover husks to local farmers for compost.

11. Stone-grind nibs in silver drums, spin with with Paraguayan cane sugar.

12. Drums hold 60 pounds of nibs, roughly equal to 384 chocolate bars.

13. Four-week aging allows chocolate tannins to relax into well-rounded flavor.

14. Careful tempering brings sheen, snap and a stabilized melting point.

15. Set final bars, packaged in lovely wrapping papers to match the flavor.

HIP HOP

A brief timeline of the genre's origins and evolution in New York

1974	South Bronx block parties, DJ Kool Herc, early "hip-hop"
1976	DJ Afrika Bambaataa battles Disco King Mario
1979	Kurtis Blow, first rapper to sign major record deal
1979	Sugarhill Gang's "Rapper's Delight"
1980	Decade of "phat" laces, dookie chains, four-finger rings
1981	The Funky 4 plus One More appear on SNL
1981	Jewish teenagers — Adam Yauch, Michael Diamond, John Berry and Kate Schellenbach — form the Beastie Boys
1982	Fresh Kid Ice [2 Live Crew] graduates from Tilden High in Brooklyn
1984	Rick Rubin and Russell Simmons form Def Jam
1985	Parental Advisory label introduced by the Recording Industry Association
1985	Childhood friends Q-Tip and Phife Dawg form A Tribe Called Quest in Queens
1985	Nike releases the Air Jordan I to the public
1986	Run-D.M.C. releases *Raising Hell*, produced by Russell Simmons and Rick Rubin
1986	The Beastie Boys release their debut album, *Licensed to Ill*
1987	DJ Scott LaRock killed outside South Bronx housing projects
1988	"Yo! MTV Raps" debuts on television
1988	Russell Simmons and Rick Rubin split
1988	KRS-One establishes the Stop the Violence Movement
1989	Spike Lee's *Do the Right Thing* with Public Enemy's "Fight the Power" as theme song
1989	*It's a Big Daddy Thing* from Bed-Stuy MC Big Daddy Kane
1990	Decade of Karl Kani, Lugz, Spike's flipped bike cap
1991	The Notorious B.I.G. featured in The Source's "Unsigned Hype" column

1992	Wu-Tang Clan forms on Staten Island
1992	Daymond John launches the clothing company FUBU
1994	2Pac shot and robbed in New York recording studio
1994	Notorious B.I.G.'s *Ready to Die* from Bad Boy Records
1995	Mobb Deep's "Shook Ones [Part II]"
1996	Bed-Stuy's Lil' Kim reaches #11 on Billboard chart
1997	Notorious B.I.G. is killed in drive-by shooting in Los Angeles
1998	*The Miseducation of Lauryn Hill* wins Grammy for Album of the Year
1998	Jay-Z releases Vol. 2...*Hard Knock Life* on Roc-A-Fella
1999	Big L is killed in a drive-by shooting in Harlem
2000	Decade of Rocawear, throwback jerseys, grillz
2001	Nas and Jay-Z public feud via Hot 97 FM face-off
2001	Puff Daddy changes name to P-Diddy
2002	Jam Master Jay shot and killed in Queens, Run-DMC disbands
2003	50 Cent's *Get Rich or Die Tryin'* goes platinum, will sell 15 million copies
2004	Fort Greene-native Ol' Dirty Bastard collapses and dies in Manhattan
2005	Lil' Kim convicted of conspiracy, perjury over involvement in HOT 97 shooting
2006	Beyoncé, Jay-Z named *Time* Magazine's most powerful couple
2011	Beginning of the Watch the Throne tour
2012	Run-D.M.C. re-forms
2012	Beastie Boy Adam "MCA" Yauch, dies of lymph node cancer at age 47
2012	Blue Ivy born
2013	Beyoncé sings Star Spangled Banner at President Obama's second inauguration
2013	Jay-Z starts sports agency, releases Magna Carta Holy Grail
2014	Twentieth anniversary of Nas' landmark album, *Illmatic*

GOLDEN ERA OF COMICS

*A sampling of characters born from the New York
comic boom of the 1930s and 40s*

SUPERHERO	POWERS
Captain Marvel	*"Shazam" grants six mythical powers*
Superman	*Flight, frozen breath, super-strength, x-ray vision, super-hearing*
Rockman	*Abyssian technology and equipment, toughness and combat skills*
The Atom	*Shape- and size-shifter who is a physicist and professor by day*
Plastic Man	*Comedic shape-shifter, loves a good joke and slapstick humor*
Human Top	*Reformed criminal, mutant, super-human ability to spin in circles*
The Whizzer	*Cobra venom and mongoose blood gives him super-human speed*
Captain America	*Super-soldier serum gives ultra-strength, endurance, reflexes*
Aquaman	*Under-water breathing, control over sea life, super-strength*
The Human Torch	*Android, fire-manipulator, fire-resistance*
Wonder Woman	*Super strength, telescopic vision, stunning beauty*
Batman	*Genius mind and espionage instincts, no supernatural shortcuts*
Green Lantern	*Green flame grants mystical powers, energy manipulation*
The Flash	*Sees the world in suspended animation, super-speed*

PARK SLOPE FOOD COOP

> *Founded in 1973, the Park Slope Food Coop is a members-only community market where all members [15,000 and counting] work 13 shifts a year at the store and receive up to 40% savings on groceries. Beyond the cheaper bill, the Coop has passionate political views, pulling Chilean grapes off the shelves during Pinochet's regime and boycotting Coca-Cola products over questionable labor practices. Below, a survey of member rules.*

DO COMPLETE YOUR SHOPPING BEFORE YOU GET ON THE CHECKOUT LINE.
Shopping while waiting on line is uncooperative.

DO UPLOAD YOUR CART ONTO THE NOSE/FRONT END OF THE CHECKOUT.
It is the shopper's responsibility to ensure that all items are unpacked and then added to the bill. Pack up your items after they have been scanned.

DO PAY IMMEDIATELY FOR CHECKED-OUT GROCERIES.
If you need an exception to this rule [to go to the ATM, for example] speak to the Shopping Squad Leader.

DO EAT ONLY PAID-FOR FOOD.
Don't nibble away at the Coop's financial health by eating food before you pay for it!

DON'T SHOP WHEN YOU ARE 'SUSPENDED' AND BEYOND YOUR 'GRACE PERIOD.'
When you come to the Coop and are told you are "suspended," you may be given a 10-day grace period at the entrance desk. During the grace period you should resolve your suspension.

DON'T ALLOW YOURSELF TO BE CHECKED OUT BY HOUSEHOLD MEMBERS OR FAMILY MEMBERS.
This will avoid the appearance of impropriety.

LEAVES OF GRASS

When Walt Whitman, a former editor of The Brooklyn Eagle newspaper, self-published his first collection of poetry, critical response ranged from incredulity to mockery to awe. Below, a sampling of the strong opinions, and, across the page, a personal note from Ralph Waldo Emerson.

Life Illustrated, 1855
It is like no other book that ever was written, and therefore, the language usually employed in notices of new publications is unavailable in describing it.

....

Criterion, 1855
It is impossible to imagine how any man's fancy could have conceived such a mass of stupid filth, unless he were possessed of the soul of a sentimental donkey that had died of disappointed love.

....

The Brooklyn Daily Times, 1855
Very devilish to some, and very divine to some, will appear these new poems, the Leaves of Grass: an attempt, as they are, of a live, naive, masculine, tenderly affectionate, rowdyish, contemplative, sensual, moral, susceptible and imperious person, to cast into literature not only his own grit and arrogance, but his own flesh and form.

The Atlantic, 1867
It is no discredit to Walt Whitman that he wrote *Leaves of Grass,* only that he did not burn it afterwards.

....

The Literary Examiner, 1856
Suppose that Mr Tupper had been banished to the backwoods...contracting a passion for the reading of Emerson and Carlyle? Suppose him maddened by this course of reading, and fancying himself not only an Emerson but an American Shakespeare to boot... In that state he would write a book exactly like Walt Whitman's *Leaves of Grass.*

....

Ezra Pound
[Whitman] is America. His crudity is an exceeding great stench, but it is America. He is the hollow place in the rock that echoes with the time. He is disgusting. He is an exceedingly nauseating pill, but he accomplishes his mission.

A NOTE FROM EMERSON

21 JULY
CONCORD, MASSTTS. 1885

Dear Sir,

I am not blind to the worth of the wonderful gift of "Leaves of Grass." I find it the most extraordinary piece of wit and wisdom that America has yet contributed. I am very happy in reading it, as great power makes us happy. It meets the demand I am always making of what seemed the sterile & stingy nature, as if too much handiwork or too much lymph in the temperament were making our western wits fat and mean. I give you joy of your free brave thought. I have great joy in it. I find incomparable things said incomparably well, as they must be. I find the courage of treatment, which so delights us, & which large perception only can inspire. I greet you at the beginning of a great career, which yet must have had a long foreground somewhere for such a start. I rubbed my eyes a little to see if this sunbeam were no illusion; but the solid sense of the book is a sober certainty. It has the best merits, namely of fortifying & encouraging. I did not know until I, last night, saw the book advertised in a newspaper, that I could trust the name as real and available for a post-office. I wish to see my benefactor, & have felt much like striking my tasks, & visiting New York to pay you my respects.

R. W. Emerson

In 1892, nearly four decades after its debut, Whitman published his "deathbed edition" of Leaves of Grass. The poet had never stopped writing and rewriting the collection, turning the twelve legendary pieces into a tome nearly 400 poems long.

THE BIG STORM

Brooklyn Preparing to Recover From Its Effects

The Brooklyn Daily Eagle
March 14, 1888

Has the blizzard begun again?

That question caused considerable alarm this morning. The morning began with a fall of very light snow. Not more than one-fourth of an inch came down, before the skies cleared and the sun came out and people looked down from their second story windows and thanks their stars that the storm was over.

They rejoiced too soon.

Very shortly after 11 o'clock the snow was coming down hard again and the sky was dark gray and threatening. The air was still and the clouds above looked full of snow.

"Say, boys!" said one jocular gentleman who stood on the steps of City Hall with a group of officials who were taking a half holiday; "if the snow does not let up the banks will rise so high that the clouds will not be able to get past."

Another steady downfall of snow is no joke. Here is what it means:

That the trains of the Long Island Railroad, laden with passengers and supplies, will be buried deeper than ever in the drifts between stations.

That the trains stuck in the drifts outside New York will share the same fate.

That Brooklyn and New York will be cut off from fresh meat, milk, butter, eggs, poultry, ducks, geese and turkeys, and fresh vegetables of all kinds.

That two or three more days of impassable drifts will find the grocery stores of the city depleted, the slaughter houses empty and half the homes of the city without food or fuel.

The supplies of these cities are never more than a week ahead of their necessities and a continuation of the storm means famine for many homes.

The disasters caused by the blizzard so far have not by any means all been chronicled. Returns from the police precincts are very meager, for communications inside the city are almost entirely interrupted. The EAGLE has already reported four cases of death from the storm, ten cases of missing people and forty cases of persons overpowered by the storm, but afterward resuscitated. The number of frostbitten amounts to many hundreds. In addition to these there must be many missing in Brooklyn and its suburbs who have not yet been reported to police by reason that the relatives are snow bound in their houses.

THE EGG CREAM

There's no more nostalgic drink for Brooklynites [especially those over 50] than the egg cream—which famously includes neither egg nor cream. It started in 1904 when Herman Fox combined milk, seltzer and his own chocolate syrup. H. Fox & Co. bottled "U-bet" syrup in 1948, and introduced egg creams to a wider audience at the 1964 World's Fair in Queens. Local diners and ice cream parlors still pour the drink. Try Junior's downtown or Tom's Restaurant in Prospect Heights or Brooklyn Farmacy in Carroll Gardens—or try to make it from scratch.

....

THE ORIGINAL EGG CREAM

(1) Pour one inch of U-bet chocolate syrup into a tall, chilled, straight-sided, 8-oz. glass.

(2) Add one inch of whole milk.

(3) Tilt the glass and spray seltzer from a pressurized cylinder off a spoon to make a robust head.

(4) Stir and drink with a straw.

JACKIE ROBINSON

The Brooklyn Daily Eagle
August 29, 1949

"I'll never forget the day when a few loudmouthed guys on the other team began to take off on Peewee Reese. They were joshing him viciously because he was playing with me and was on the field nearby. Mind you, they were not yelling at me; I suppose they did not have the nerve to do that, but they were calling him some very vile names and every one bounced off Peewee and hit me like a machine-gun bullet. Peewee kind of sensed the sort of hopeless, dead feeling in me and came over and stood beside me for a while. He didn't say a word but he looked over at the chaps who were yelling at me through him and just stared. He was standing by me. I could tell you that. Slowly, the jibes died down like when you kill a snake an inch at a time, and then there was nothing but quiet from them. It was wonderful the way this little guy did it. I will never forget it. All the fellows on the Dodger team have worked with me in the same spirit."

SUPERNATURAL

Mollie Fancher suffered a terrible fall from an electric trolley car in 1865, after which she lost her senses of sight and touch, went weeks without eating, and confined herself to bed in Fort Greene. When Mollie later claimed to have supernatural powers, newspapers called her the "Brooklyn Enigma." Several of those mysterious claim are listed below.

- ☞ Read unopened letters.
- ☞ Describe articles hidden in pockets.
- ☞ Tell time from her small gold watch, hanging across the room.
- ☞ Read books hidden under her sheets.
- ☞ Speak with the dead.
- ☞ Observe her friends in the outside world, recounting details from their days.

CHESS

> **"HIGH SCHOOL
> STUDENT, BOBBY
> FISCHER WINS
> U.S. CHESS
> CHAMPIONSHIP"**

New York Daily News
January 9, 1958

Brooklyn has itself a new triple crown winner today. What Duke Snider and Roy Campanella are to baseball, 14-year-old Bobby Fischer is to the world of chess. Chess fans about the country are calling Bobby "player of the century" and "greatest chess prodigy of the age."

At a tournament completed early yesterday, at the Manhattan Chess Club, the smooth-cheeked sophomore from Erasmus Hall HS won the United States Chess Championship with a score topping 13 of the very best players in the country. With the junior championship won last July in San Francisco and the open championship garnered in August in Cleveland, Bobby today is undisputed king of the ancient sport, and probably the only player to have held all three titles at one time.

Although Bobby was not announced winner until well after midnight and he did not get back to his home at 560 Lincoln Place until 2 A.M., he attended school as usual yesterday, apparently unruffled by his unparalleled achievement. Bobby's next step is the world championship to held in Yugoslavia next September. Bobby and another member of the American team will make the trip if sufficient funds can be raised to cover their expenses.

Bobby was to have played in Russia last summer but financial support for the tour was pledged too late. The boy turned down a bid to compete against a group of the world's chess masters at the Christmas tournament at Hastings, England, in favor of the Manhattan tourney...

The strain of the Lessing J. Rosenwald Trophy tournament, as the masters championship is called, has been severe, according to Mrs. Fischer, and Bobby was anxious to forget chess and concentrate on his studies and on other interests — tennis, swimming, skiing and the like.

But chances are the lustre added by his latest win will bring in another spate of invitations for further exhibitions. Talk of a trip to Russia has begun again and the State Department is said to be trying to raise the money.

SPECIAL NOTICE, WANTS AND MISCELLANY

The Brooklyn Daily Eagle
July 26, 1855

BONE DUST.---FOR SALE, a pure article of bone, of a variety of fineness, from half inch to perfect powder, a great article for Grape vines or farming purposes. Apply to J.S. Mackey, 6 Court street, Brooklyn

LET THERE BE LIGHT, AND THERE was light — now if you wish to get pure Burning Fluid. Camphene and Alcohol; also the best sperm, solar, lard and whale oil, call at Chappel & Co, 63 Fulton st. Wholesale and Retail Dealers. N. B.- Girandoles and Lamps repaired, altered and regilded.

TO NERVOUS SUFFERERS. — Rev. John M. Dagnall's celebrated IGNATIA PILLS, for the effectual cure of Nervous Weakness and Nervous Complaints of every kind, prepared by his own dispenser from his invaluable prescription, may now be obtained of all druggists. Agents for Brooklyn — MRS. Hayes, 175 Fulton-st. ; T. MARSELL-US, 192 Court-st. ; D. OWEN, 154 Atlantic-st.

TO THE LADIES.
As the month of May is the time for changing houses, and the woods and flowery vallies are filled with the little songsters, so is DODGE & CO.'S STORE. Nos. 812 and 314 Fulton street. With the latest styles of FANCY BIRD CAGES, which they offer at lower prices than any other store in Brooklyn. Please call and select for yourselves.

TEETH ! TEETH !! TEETH !!! — N.B. GRIFFIN, Dental Surgeon, 276 Fulton-st. Brooklyn, would make known to the public, that he is enabled to furnish artificial teeth of superior quality of every size and color.

- ☞ *Gold Atmospheric Plates for.....$60.00*
- ☞ *Partial setts per tooth from.....3.00 to 4.00*
- ☞ *Cavities filled with Gold from.....0.50 to 1.00*
- ☞ *Full upper and under setts on Silver.....20.00*
- ☞ *Filling with Tin Foil or Cement.....0.50*
- ☞ *Extracting.....0.25*

THE NEW YORK GARBAGEMAN

E.B. White

There is no one in all New York that we envy more than the garbageman. Not even a fireman gets so much fun out of life. The jolly, jolly garbageman goes banging down the street without a thought for anyone. He clatters his cans as he listenth; he scatters on the winds with never a thought that the windblown ash problem was settled in 1889 when the little old one-horse dump carts had covers put on them. He is shrewd in measuring his pace, and goes down the block bit by bit, innocently keeping just to windward of you. He drives like a ward boss through red lights and green, and backs his truck over the crossing with more privilege than a baby carriage on Fifth Avenue. He is as masterful as a pirate and chock-full of gusto. As we watch a garbage crew at work, we momentarily expect to see them burst into song and clink property beakers. Why shouldn't they? They have the town by the tail and they know it.

*Published by
The New Yorker on
December 6, 1930*

CLASSES

The diverse world of how-to in Brooklyn

SANDHOGS

When the Brooklyn Bridge was built, Surgeon of the Bridge Company, Dr. Andrew Smith, made nine rules to protect diggers called "sandhogs" from debilitating physical effects of compromised air.

SMITH'S NINE RULES

(1) Never enter the caisson with an empty stomach.

(2) Use as far as possible a meat diet, and take warm coffee freely.

(3) Always put on extra clothing on coming out, and avoid exposure to cold.

(4) Exercise as little as may be during the first hour coming out, and lie down if possible.

(5) Use intoxicating liquors sparingly; better not at all.

(6) Take at least eight hours' sleep every night.

(7) See that the bowels are open every day.

(8) Never enter the caisson if at all sick.

(9) Report at once at the office all cases of illness, even if they occur after going home.

STREET GANGS

Notorious Brooklyn affiliations in the 1970s

⊳ Tomahawks	⊳ Dirty Ones	⊳ Wicked Ones
⊳ Young Barons	⊳ Young Survivors	⊳ Black Attacks
⊳ Pure Hell	⊳ Black Stabbers	⊳ Black Bulls
⊳ Warlords	⊳ Trouble Bros.	⊳ Unknown Riders
⊳ Vanguards	⊳ Outlaws	⊳ Sinners
⊳ Savage Nomads	⊳ Excons	⊳ Mad Caps
⊳ Phantom Lords	⊳ Latin Tops	⊳ Spanish Kings

SHEEPSHEAD BAY

Brooklyn's quaint fishing village was once home to 50-plus "party boats," vessels that allowed anyone to hop aboard with rod and reel. As pollution increased, interest waned, and most of the fishing operations folded. However, one of the oldest Sheepshead Bay families still operate their Dorothy B. fleet, circa 1918.

DOROTHY B. #1

In 1918 William Bradshaw bought a small boat—sea air was said to be good for the lead paint in his lungs—named it "Dorothy B." after his first daughter, and docked it along Emmons Avenue.

....

DOROTHY B. #2 AND #3

In the late 20s the Bradshaws grew their fleet, each vessel bigger than the previous. They charged fifty cents for a ride, and according to William's son, Walter, "for fifty cents you'd catch a sack full of fish that was enough to feed your family for a week."

....

DOROTHY B. #4

Business was good enough in 1931 that the family purchased a 45-footer, taking fishermen out onto the Atlantic Ocean for runs of fluke, mackerel, blues, cod, porgy, striped bass and blackfish.

DOROTHY B. #5

By 1950 William's sons—Joe, Frank and Walter—were running the fishing business full-time, and bought a stately boat that fit more than two dozen people.

....

DOROTHY B. #6

A sleek, 83-foot converted World War II subchaser became the pride of their fleet. In 1974 Joe, Frank, and Walter retired and sold to Walter's son, Kevin.

....

DOROTHY B. #7

In 1980 Captain Kevin bought the seventh Dorothy B. and broke with tradition by including "VII" in the name.

....

DOROTHY B #8

The family's first aluminum boat is also the fastest and biggest, at 90-feet long. In 2009, Captain Kevin decided to move his business to Atlantic Highlands, New Jersey.

PARK SLOPE PLANE CRASH

December 16, 1960, began as an ordinary day in Park Slope. The corner of Seventh Avenue and Sterling Place was as picturesque as ever. All that changed shortly before 11 a.m., when United Airlines Flight 826 collided mid-air with Trans World Airlines Flight 266, crashing into the neighborhood. Six bystanders on the ground were killed, as were all 128 passengers. The fire commissioner called it "an act of God" that the major impact of the crash had been on a vacant church rather than on surrounding buildings. One high school teacher told the New York Herald Tribune that he could see the pilots' faces from his classroom window just before the plane crashed. One young boy, a passenger named Stephen Baltz, was thrown from the plane and landed in a snowbank. He survived for only one day, but recounted to his rescuers on Seventh Avenue that just before the plane went down, he noticed the snow falling in Brooklyn. "It looked like a picture out of a fairy book," he said.

CRIME

Selected statistics from an 1870 annual police report for the city of Brooklyn

OFFENSES AND TOTAL ARRESTS FOR THE YEAR

Bastardy..47
Bigamy..8
Cruelty To Animals................138
Disobeying Parents....................1
Highway Robbery...................40
Insulting Females.......................9
Keeping Disorderly Houses.....20
Lounging................................507
Malicious Mischief..............433
Seduction...................................21
Sneak Thieving........................19
Vagrancy..............................1,463

OCCUPATIONS OF THOSE ARRESTED

Boot-Blacks 26
Cigar-Makers..........................127
Errand Boys 30
Ferry Master............................. 1
House-Keepers 2,347
Icemen......................................10
Japanners....................................7
Morocco-Dressers...................29
Organ Grinders 2
Oyster Dealers............................6
Rag Pickers 21
Servants................................1,251

HENRY WARD BEECHER

Throughout his years at Plymouth Church in Brooklyn Heights, abolitionist preacher Henry Ward Beecher gave rousing speeches championing women's suffrage and the theory of evolution, even using the pulpit to purchase the freedom of a nine-year-old slave girl, Sally Marie Diggs. Controversy was Beecher's truest companion. As his lectures were published and sold throughout the country, Beecher became well known, but his fame peaked in 1875 when he stood trial for having an affair with a former colleague's wife.

In his own words:

ON SCIENCE
"The future is not in danger from the revelations of science. Science is truth; Truth loves the truth."

ON EQUALITY
"If any man says to me, 'Why will you agitate the woman's question, when it is the hour for the black man?' I answer, it is the hour for every man, black or white."

ON VOTING RIGHTS
"The truth that I have to urge is not that women have the right of suffrage—not that Chinamen or Irishmen...not that native born Yankees have the right of suffrage—but that suffrage is the inherent right of mankind."

ON EVOLUTION
"In respect to the fantastic notions that we sprang from monkeys...It is not where a man starts, it is where he ends."

ON CHRISTIANITY
"If the American people are ever driven away from the Church, and from faith in the Christian religion, it will be the fault of the Church and of the Pulpit."

AMUSEMENTS

*A small selection of Coney Island attractions found at
Sea-Lion Park, Steeplechase, Luna Park and independent
proprietors from the late 1800s to 1960s.*

Culver's Steel Tower

Thompson's Switchback Railway

Dreamland Circus Sideshow

Shoot-the-Chutes

Flip Flap

Razzle Dazzle Swing

Earthquake Floor

The Human Cage

House Upside Down

Human Roulette Wheel

A Trip to the Moon

War of the Worlds

Infant Incubators

Dragon's Gorge

Drop the Dips

Witching Waves

Aqua Girls

Creation and Hell Gate

Wormwood's Monkey Circus

Congress of Curious People

The Sacrifice Biblical Show

Mack's Electric Fish Pond

Palace of Electricity

Flip Flap Railway

Loop-the-Loop

Jackman's Thriller

The Giant Racer

The Cyclone

Parachute Tower

The Big Dipper

Tunnel of Love

Drop the Dips

Thunderbolt

Tornado Roller Coaster

Wonder Wheel

Barrel of Fun

Cages of Wild Wolves

Ghost Hole

Helter Skelter

Spook-a-Rama

BAD ELEPHANT KILLED

*TOPSY MEETS QUICK AND PAINLESS
DEATH AT CONEY ISLAND*

The Commercial Advertiser
January 5, 1903

Topsy, the ill-tempered Coney Island elephant, was put to death in Luna Park, Coney Island, yesterday afternoon. The execution was witnessed by 1,500 or more curious persons, who went down to the island to see the end of the huge beast, to whom they had fed peanuts and cakes in summer that are gone. In order to make Topsy's execution quick and sure 460 grams of cyanide of potassium were fed to her in carrots. Then a hawser was put around her neck and one end attached to a donkey engine and the other end to a post. Next wooden sandals lined with copper were attached to her feet. These electrodes were connected by copper wire with the Edison electric light plant and a current of 6,600 volts was sent through her body. The big beast died without a trumpet or a grown.

Topsy was brought to this country twenty-eight years ago by the Forepaugh Circus, and has been exhibited throughout the United States. She was ten feet high and 19 feet 11 inches length. Topsy developed a bad temper two years ago and killed two keepers in Texas. Last spring, when the Forepaugh show was in Brooklyn, J. F. Blount, a keeper, tried to feed a lighted cigarette to her. She picked him up with her trunk and dashed him to the ground, killing him instantly.

Adding a twist to the macabre affair, filmmakers from the Edison Manufacturing Company captured Topsy's demise in a 74-second silent film titled, "Electrocuting an Elephant." They released it 13 days after the killing and showed it on coin-operated kinetoscopes.

MAPS

Hand-illustrated maps to tell stories about the borough's finest restaurants, hip hop heritage, literary life, where art thrives, where kids play and where to find peace and quiet.

Vinegar Hill
House

Fort
Defiance

Frankies
Sputino

⫸ NEW INSTITUTIONS ⫷

From trattorias to open-air cafes to a reclaimed dining car, these beloved neighborhood favorites will stand the test of time.

DINER (1998)

This refurbished 1920s dining car has been feeding Williamsburg's creative set since 1998. The verbal menu changes nightly, with the exception of an excellent grass-fed burger. *85 Broadway, dinernyc.com*

FETTE SAU (2007)

No waiters, no menus, no plates: Just trays of carefully sourced and patiently smoked meat in a barbecue style all its own. *354 Metropolitan Ave, fettesaubbq.com*

FORT DEFIANCE (2009)

Friendly staff, NYC's best muffuletta, a happy brunch crowd. *365 Van Brunt St, fortdefiance-brooklyn.com*

FRANKIES 457 SPUNTINO (2004)

Elevated takes on cucina nonna classics: eggplant parm, fluffy meatballs, brown sage butter cavatelli, and killer Sunday gravy. *457 Court St, frankiesspuntino.com*

JAMES (2008)

A neighborhood restaurant if your neighbor is Alice Waters, maybe. The menu is seasonally driven, but with enough standards to make it a weeknight hang. *289 Flatbush Ave, jamesrestaurantny.com*

LOCANDA VINI E OLII (2001)

This repurposed pharmacy set the tone for what every trendy Italian restaurant in Brooklyn would soon emulate: small, thoughtful pastas; rustic Tuscan mains, and a wine list of excellent small producers. *129 Gates Ave, locandany.com*

VINEGAR HILL HOUSE (2008)

On a quiet street near the Navy Yards, their honest wood-fire cooking matches the restaurant's historic charm — natural-born rather than manufactured. The cast-iron chicken is your move. *72 Hudson Ave, vinegarhillhouse.com*

LOCAL EXPERT *Short Stack Editions know well the key ingredients to restaurants. Their series of micro-cookbooks [Honey, Lemons, Tomatoes, etc] are beautiful works of art. shortstackeditions.com*

≫ LITERATURE ≪

Ever since Walt Whitman walked the streets, Brooklyn has been a writer's [and reader's] haven.

FRANKLIN PARK READING SERIES

This Crown Heights garage-turned-bar becomes into a literary salon on the second Monday of each month. Past participants include Mary Gaitskill, Jennifer Egan and Colson Whitehead. *618 St. John's Place, franklinparkbrooklyn.com*

BROOKLYN PUBLIC LIBRARY

The columned Central Branch of the Brooklyn Public Library looks majestic at its perch in Grand Army Plaza; inside are author talks and panels in addition to sci-fi film screenings and chamber music concerts. *10 Grand Army Plaza, bklynlibrary.org*

826NYC & THE BROOKLYN SUPERHERO SUPPLY CO.

At this nonprofit clubhouse, tutors teach kids and teens how to write. Also a go-to catchall for aspiring caped crusaders. *372 Fifth Ave, 826nyc.org*

BOOKCOURT

The platonic ideal of an indie bookshop: Robust reading series, obscure staff recommendations and a comfy children's section. *163 Court St, bookcourt.com*

GREENLIGHT

Fort Greene's beloved bookstore has launched many local partnerships, from a kiosk at BAM to an African-American reading series at Bedford Stuyvesant Restoration. *686 Fulton St, greenlightbookstore.com*

BROOKLYN INN

When Jonathan Ames's HBO show *Bored to Death* was canceled, he threw a going-away party at this century-old hangout. *148 Hoyt St*

BROOKLYN BOOK FESTIVAL

Every September literary stars and book nerds descend on downtown Brooklyn. *brooklynbookfestival.org*

LOCAL EXPERTS *Brooklyn is home to several upstart journals including N+1, Electric Literature, A Public Space, Tin House and One Story, which publishes a single short story every three weeks.*

Norman Mailer

Book Court

Brooklyn Inn

826 Brooklyn Superhero Supply

Walt Whitman

Greenlight Bookstore

A Tree Grows in Brooklyn

Brooklyn Public Library

Franklin Park Reading Series

Westinghouse High

Albee Square Mall

Adam Yauch Park

BIZ MARKIE

Countryhouse Diner

R.I.P. MCA

Brooklyn Hip Hop Festival

Marcy Projects

Chapelle's Block Party

Do The Right Thing

⋙ HIP HOP ⋘

From Biggie to the Beastie Boys to Spike Lee joints,
Brooklyn's influence on hip hop culture runs deep.

ADAM YAUCH PARK

Tucked under the BQE, this Brooklyn Heights playground was renamed in memory of the Beastie Boy who grew up around the corner.

....

MARCY HOUSES

The Bed-Stuy public housing complex serves as the setting for many a Jay Z song about childhood and early forays into both hustling and rap.

....

COUNTRY HOUSE DINER

"A T-bone steak, cheese eggs, and Welch's grape," from Notorious B.I.G.'s song "Big Poppa" was a shout out to this diner, down the street from 226 St. James Place, his childhood home in Clinton Hill.

....

WESTINGHOUSE HIGH SCHOOL

Downtown vocational school better known for lunchroom battles of freestylin' students like DMX, Busta Rhymes and others.

ALBEE SQUARE MALL

"My house is the Albee Square Mall," sings T.J. Swan on the classic Biz Markie track, written by Big Daddy Kane and named after this long-gone Brooklyn mall.

....

BROKEN ANGEL HOUSE

Featured as the backdrop for Dave Chappelle's "Block Party" film, featuring performances by Brooklyn's Mos Def, Talib Kweli, Dead Prez, and the re-united Fugees.

....

DO THE RIGHT THING

Spike Lee's epic Brooklyn joint shot mostly in Bed-Stuy, and gave a 19-year-old dancer and choreographer named Rosie Perez her first movie role.

....

BROOKLYN HIP HOP FESTIVAL

Established in 2005, the BHF is NYC's largest cultural event with Hip Hop at the core. Performances, panel discussions, exhibits, and more.

LOCAL EXPERT *Famed entertainment lawyer and MTV VP, Reggie Ossé founded "The Combat Jack Show," a weekly Brooklyn podcast about hip hop culture and current events. thecombatjackshow.com*

⇻ KIDS ⇺

From stroller-slammed Park Slope to Coney Island's Cyclone, this borough is chockablock with children—and ways to keep them entertained.

PROSPECT PARK

At the Zucker Natural Exploration Area playground, kids play in hollowed-out stumps and balance-beam logs created from some of the 500 trees felled by Hurricane Sandy. 31 *East Dr, prospectpark.org*

BROOKLYN BOTANIC GARDEN

Brooklyn Botanic is the perfect picnic destination—kids run through cherry blossoms in the spring and dried leaves in the fall. The immersive Children's Discovery Garden reopens in June 2015 after a two-year expansion. 150 *Eastern Parkway, bbg.org*

JANE'S CAROUSEL

French architect Jean Nouvel enclosed a 1922 carousel in an ultramodern glass shed, which now sits on the East River as part of the fantasyland [giant soccer fields, beaches, playgrounds] that is Brooklyn Bridge Park. *janescarousel.com*

NEW YORK TRANSIT MUSEUM

At this underground 1936 subway station, children board vintage subway and elevated cars. *Boerum Pl and Schermerhorn*

BROOKLYN FARMACY & SODA FOUNTAIN

Opened in 2010, Cobble Hill has embraced this throwback, especially the maple egg creams. Stop by on Friday nights for live kids' music. 513 *Henry St*

CONEY ISLAND

Hot dogs, roller coasters, the boardwalk, a mermaid parade, the Brooklyn Aquarium and an amazingly fun minor league baseball team—Coney Island is a summer paradise.

SLODYCZE WEDEL

Poland has a candy tradition that rivals Switzerland's, as evidenced in this chocolate-filled, well-priced candy store in the heart of Polish Greenpoint. 772 *Manhattan Ave*

> **LOCAL EXPERTS** *Marcos Stafne, PhD, is the mind behind visitor experience at the fantastic Brooklyn Children's Museum, built in 1899 and the first of its kind. 145 Brooklyn Ave, brooklynkids.org*

Jane's Carousel

New York Transit Musuem

Brooklyn Farmacy

Coney Island!

Luna Park

Słodycze
Wedel

Brooklyn Children's
Musuem

Brooklyn Botanic Gardens

Storefront
Ten Eyck

Centotto

Clearing

The Bog Art

BOGART ST

GRATTAN ST

Bushwick
Art + Shipping

Silent
Barn

⋙ BUSHWICK ART ⋘

*Emerging talent, warehouse studios, fantastic graffiti —
this neighborhood stokes the borough's creative spirit.*

CENTOTTO
Writer and artist Paul D'Agostino's own living room doubles as a gallery, where he hosts rotating exhibits and what artist conversations he calls *interstizios*. *250 Moore St, #108, centotto.com*

CLEARING GALLERY
French artist Olivier Babin moved his Brooklyn outpost to a 5,000-square-foot former truck repair depot. Since 2011, Babin has become a noted eye for new talent. *396 Johnson Avenue*

ROBERTA'S
This standout pizzeria put the Bushwick dining scene on the map—or at least, got Manhattanites to make the trek. Pairs perfectly with a gallery opening. Also on site: Heritage Radio Network, which broadcasts food-focused programming five days a week. *261 Moore St; robertaspizza.com*

STOREFRONT TEN EYCK
A champion for emerging Bushwick artists, community activist Deborah Brown reigns over this massive, sky-lit industrial space. Exhibit openings are packed. *324 Ten Eyck St, storefrontteneyck.com*

THE BOGART
One-stop shop for galleries and studios. Check out Mellow Pages, a library/reading room filled with limited-edition books. *56 Bogart St, 56bogartstreet.com*

BUSHWICK ART AND SHIPPING
The neighborhood canvas-and-supply shop also organizes panels, concerts, and art shows in its courtyard. *1053 Flushing Ave, bushwickartandshipping.com*

SILENT BARN
'Zine fairs. A "makeout" fest. A resident theatre company. No event is off limits at this DIY collective, run by 70-plus volunteers. *603 Bushwick Ave, silentbarn.org*

LOCAL EXPERT *The three-day Bushwick Open Studios festival unofficially kicks off the summer season. It's the biggest event of its kind in New York City. artsinbushwick.org*

⫸ ESCAPES ⫷

*Finding peace and quiet in New York's
most populous borough*

PROSPECT PARK

This 536-acre green space—
designed by Frederick Law
Olmstead and Calvert Vaux of
Central Park fame—is a magnet
for joggers, hikers, birders,
and anyone looking to forget
they live in a concrete jungle.
prospectpark.org

....

BROOKLYN HEIGHTS PROMENADE

This one-third-mile-long walk-
way overlooking the East River
and lower Manhattan is maybe
the best view in all of NYC.
Our advice: Pack a book, grab a
bench, and turn off your phone.
Joralemon St. and Grace Ct.

....

LOUIS VALENTINO JR. PARK

Though simple, this charming
park in Red Hook gets you as
close to the Statue of Liberty
as possible in Brooklyn. There's
a pier that juts out over the
water—an ideal perch for
breezy sunset views. *Coffey and
Ferris streets*

NORTH BROOKLYN BOAT CLUB

Tucked into an alley in a not-so-
scenic part of Greenpoint, this
boathouse gives paddlers access
to hidden beaches or crowdless
water-roaming in Newtown
Creek. *49 Ash Street, northbrook-
lynboatclub.org*

....

GREEN-WOOD CEMETERY

Stunning Gothic arches lead
to the resting place of notable
New Yorkers—F.A.O. Schwartz,
Boss Tweed, and Jean-Michel
Basquiat among them. [Not
to mention the colonies of
blue-green monk parrots.] It's
wonderfully tranquil—hills and
valleys, glacial ponds and war
monuments. *500 25th Street,
green-wood.com*

....

MANHATTAN BEACH PARK

The quiet crescent is on the
same peninsula as crowd-heavy
Coney Island—but it's much the
opposite in vibe. *Oriental Blvd.
between Ocean and Mackenzie*

LOCAL EXPERT *Mermaid Spa is the borough's best Russian banya.
Eucalyptus steams, icy baths, dried-birch veniks — and maybe a shot
of vodka. 3703 Mermaid Ave, seagatebaths.com*

Brooklyn
Heights
Promenade

Louis
Valentino
Jr. Park

Take the **B**
to Brighton Beach

Manhattan
Beach
Park

Green-Wood
Cemetery

North
Brooklyn
Boat Club

Prospect Park

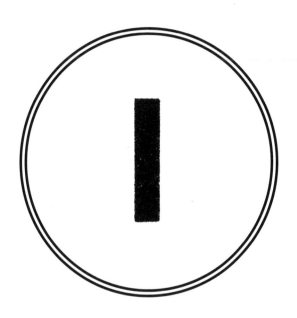

INTERVIEWS

*Fifteen conversations about high school basketball, the
immigrant experience, making violins, running a bar,
working with Spike Lee and more.*

⋙ KENNY PRETLOW ⋘

BASKETBALL COACH

COACHING AT Lincoln High is like Broadway versus off Broadway. There's a big difference.

STEPHAN MARBURY, Lance Stevenson, Sebastian Telfair. They all grew up in the projects. And they used their talent to get out.

I THINK EVERY KID in Coney Island aspires to be the next one to make it.

EVERY YEAR, [former head coach] Tiny Morton would say, "We're not defending a championship." You have new kids every year.

THE MOST underrated skill in basketball is the ability to read the floor.

THE GAME'S CHANGED since the 80s. Today, they all want to shoot 3's. And there aren't many real low post players.

THE BEST New York City player I've ever seen was Kenny Anderson.

I REMEMBER Lance Stevenson in the borough championship game against Boys High. We were down 15 points and he said, "Give me the ball 'cause I'm about to bust these guys." He scored 15 straight and then assisted on the game winner.

MY GREAT-GRANDPARENTS came to Brooklyn in the 1930s.

CRACK WAS really, really, really bad in the housing developments. I saw it firsthand.

I STAYED IN Williamsburg with my grandmother a lot. She made homemade biscuits from scratch. Eggs, flour, and love, she said.

MY NUMBER ONE job is not winning championships. It's graduating each and every one of my players.

WE HAVE TO exercise our minds like we exercise our bodies.

I NEVER GET tired of the grind of basketball. Never.

MARTY MARKOWITZ

BOROUGH LEADER

THE BROOKLYN where I grew up was *Father Knows Best*. We rode bicycles. We played stickball. We made scooters out of milk cartons. We would play Skully with soda caps.

· ·

I LIVED TWO and a half blocks from Ebbets Field.

· ·

MY FATHER WAS a waiter in a kosher delicatessen. He died when I was 9.

· ·

MY MOTHER WAS a horrible cook. I hate to say that but it's true. When I got my first taste of Italian food, I fell in love.

· ·

ATLANTIC YARDS? I can't tell you how many ups and downs we had. They felt that I was a bum, a crook. It didn't make sense. Why would I do anything to harm Brooklyn?

· ·

I WENT INTO public service to put a smile on everyone's face.

· ·

SEPTEMBER 11 was primary day, so I was out front of a school in Prospect Heights giving out leaflets, and then I heard a thud.

· ·

THEN THE second plane hit. I immediately called my wife.

· ·

WHO DO WE KNOW? Who do we know? Who do we know?

· ·

I NEVER WANTED to live in Manhattan. That doesn't mean that it's not exciting and pulsating. It is! But there's just something about Brooklyn.

· ·

MANHATTAN IS THE third largest borough.

· ·

GIULIANI WAS very tough. You do it my way or the highway.

· ·

BLOOMBERG WAS first a businessman. Everything had to be quantified and qualified. He wasn't a kind of huggy-hugyy-kissy-kissy kind of guy.

· ·

BILL DE BLASIO, his heart's in the right place.

· ·

YOU CAN'T win them all. You try, but you can't.

⫸ HANNAH TINTI ⫷

WRITER AND EDITOR

I HAVE five jobs. You want to hear about them?

I'M EDITOR-IN-CHIEF of One Story. I teach a workshop at NYU. I teach at Columbia. I teach a class at the Museum of Natural History that combines science and writing. And I run a conference in Italy every year called Sirenland.

I ALSO HAVE a book under contract that's due right about now, so that's my other job.

WE LAUNCHED *One Story* in 2002. We mail one great short story every three weeks.

I MOVED OVER to Gowanus when I was evicted from my six-floor walkup in the Lower East Side of Manhattan.

ARTISTS GO wherever the rent is cheap. Then they make the area interesting and cool and diverse, so people want to move there, and then all the artists have to leave. Staten Island is the final frontier.

EVERY YEAR we host a spoof on a debutante ball. It's about 500 people, and we present One Story writers who've published their first book that year.

IT'S HARD to be a writer and to actually live here. Writers helping writers—that's the only way to make it.

LITERARY AGENTS are like real estate agents. It's not 250 square feet; it's cozy. It's their job to lie.

I PLAY POKER with a group of writers. Colson Whitehead, Nathan Englander, Myla Goldberg. Colson is the best.

CONTRADICTION IS what makes things interesting.

I LOVE Gowanus. Seven years of walking past decay and the Canal, the medical waste and syphilis in the water. It's desolate, and there's a silence. It's where I get moments of contemplation.

THERE WERE swans living out there for a while.

≫ ROSIE PEREZ ≪

ACTRESS

I LIVED IN North Bushwick with my aunt. She worked two factory jobs, one as a garment seamstress and one in the fried pork rind factory.

OUR WHOLE BLOCK would go to Coney Island together. One sweaty, hot subway car. Those were the days of boom boxes, so you'd yell out, "Change the channel! Change the channel!"

CENTRAL PARK, it's beautiful, but you go there and it's so vast. And you don't know anyone.

THAT'S WHY I moved back.

PEOPLE FAULT ME and Spike for opening our big mouths about Brooklyn. We should have kept them shut!

WHEN MY MOTHER put me in the system, I had to be in a convent with nuns. And while I was there I was dreaming of home. Brooklyn was where my happiness was.

THE NUNS put on plays and they always put me in the lead part.

IT NEVER OCCURRED to me to be a career choice—until the day I met Spike Lee in a nightclub. He said, "You're an actress," and I said, "No, I'm not."

BUT, OH MY GOD, the nuns knew.

WHEN I FIRST went to the Barclays Center, I saw every color of the rainbow. It wasn't all whitewashed. It was kids from the neighborhood. One of them said, "Ms. Perez, are you OK?" I said, "Where are you from?" The guy goes, well, I live in East Flatbush. My family's been there for years. And I just started bawling.

TO ME, it's a beautiful thing that I've come full circle and I'm still living here. I'm still living within my happiness in my Brooklyn.

MY CUP runneth over. It's just been too good.

»»» BRANDON STANTON ««

PHOTOGRAPHER AND BLOGGER

I'VE BEEN interviewing people for *Humans of New York* since 2011. Every day. That's about 10,000 portraits.

THE BIGGEST learning curve was dealing with the no's.

WHEN SOMEONE walks up to you, a stranger, a blank slate—no opinion, no judgement—then you are able to share your thoughts with more abandon.

WHAT'S YOUR biggest fear? What's the biggest mistake you've ever made? What do you feel most guilty about?

I'M AWARE of how uncomfortable it is. It's terrifying.

THE FEELING OF being heard is always stronger than the fear of being revealed.

IT'S NOT ABOUT what I say. It's about the energy that I'm giving off.

AND IT'S TEN TIMES easier on 60-degree days.

NORMALLY I'LL DECIDE where to go five minutes before I walk out of my apartment.

A MOSQUE down the street that woke me up with a call to prayer. Waking up with a shouting match outside my window. Bedford-Stuyvesant, I love it so much.

HALF OF the blog is Bed-Stuy.

TWELVE MILLION on Facebook, 2.8 million on Instagram. It's about the stories.

TO ME, it's the diversity. It's the range of human experience that's on the streets.

EVERYTHING ON the Internet is ephemeral.

NEW YORK CITY feels like a small town to me.

TEN THOUSAND PEOPLE have told me the deepest stories of their life. It can't help but open your mind and make you a more accepting person.

⋙ ANTONIO "SUNNY" BALZANO ⋘

BAR OWNER

I WAS BORN right next door—in 1934—and I still live there.

....

IN THOSE DAYS Sunny's was called John's Bar and Restaurant. My uncle owned it. But my father, my aunts and uncles, everybody was working there.

....

SUNNY'S ISN'T mine. It's ours.

....

BACK THEN, if you looked out on the river—the ships there—it was like the Long Island Expressway. Ships on each side of each pier. So right across the street were fifteen or twenty thousand people working.

....

COME LUNCHTIME, they'd fill up the place.

....

I HAD A VERY bad case of dyslexia, so I was never a good student. They just thought you were stupid.

....

BUT THERE WAS one thing I could do. I could draw.

....

I HAD AN AUNT who was near-blind in one eye and had a glass eye in the other. I remember being a child and she was able to hold my drawings up to her face, up to her good eye, and go, Come si bella! Then she would travel through the building, showing everyone what I did.

....

I REMEMBER the ice man. He was a debtor. One day he was filling the ice one morning, and I was sleeping in the front room here. Bang, bang. I look out and his body is laying on the sidewalk, blood dripping down the curb.

....

THAT WAS MY first experience with that.

....

INSTEAD OF shooting rabbits, we shot bottles. One day we decided to play quick-draw. I thought: I've got a quicker way. And I stick the gun in the holster and cock back the hammer. I say one, two, three, and he throws the bottle. I grab the handle and I shoot myself. Right through the leg. Cut the artery in half. I was bleeding like a pig.

ONE DAY I found a Cezanne painting in the street with bullet holes in it.

IT WAS RAINING that day, and it began to peel away from its backing. I liked it, so I brought it in. I began to fill in the bullet holes with toilet paper. I had watercolors and I restored it. I still have it. It's upstairs.

I REMEMBER Andy Warhol came to me once and he said, "Sunny, I would like you to be in one of my movies." I said, "Andy, I really appreciate the offer, but I wouldn't want my mother to see it."

PEOPLE ALWAYS want your attention. But if you're bartending, and someone's talking to you, you always have an excuse.

BEING BEHIND the bar, you're visible yet invisible. There is something sweet about that.

IN FACT, I just recently grew this mustache. I was thinking it could be a disguise.

I HAVE REINS on it. But sometimes the reins break, and the horses run wild. I don't want it to get so wild that I don't recognize it.

RED HOOK could be at the end of Montauk. It's a little village.

THE MORNING OF Sandy, I don't know where they all came from, but volunteers showed up with pumps to pump out the basement, men to refurbish the floor. They saved it.

I JOINED THE boxing club when I was a kid. I won some, but that didn't make a difference. I was willing to get up there and fight. It's all those things—being in that ring, lights shining, all these folks around watching you—I think it was all preparation to do this.

Sunny's Bar is located at 253 Conover Street in Red Hook. It's open every day but Monday. The Saturday bluegrass jam starts at 10 pm. sunnysredhook.com

⫸ SAWAKO OKOCHI ⫷

CHEF

I WAS a picky eater.

AS A CHILD, I was always left alone at the dinner table. Sometimes I'd sit there for an hour looking at my plate.

WE MOVED TO Texas from Japan.

SCHOOL FOOD was a big disappointment. That led me to start cooking on my own.

I DECIDED to go to culinary school in New York. Everything about the city was surprising—dirty streets and subways, and everybody walked. I got tired a lot.

WHEN MY HUSBAND I started dating, we were both unemployed. We spent the whole summer hanging out.

ONE DAY he was at the Brooklyn library looking at archives of old Jewish restaurants and he came across a place called Shalom Japan. The name stayed with us.

WE KNEW it'd be hard.

NORMAL DAYS, I check inventory on pastry first and make what's needed. Then I test recipes with Aaron and help the cooks if needed. We have a staff meal, then daily meeting and go into service.

WHO WOULD THINK about putting a lox bowl with sushi rice?

SAKE KASU CHALLAH. Toro toasts with scallion cream cheese. Mochi ice cream blitzes. And Aaron's matzoh ramen.

FOOD MAKES people happy.

YOU GET AN OLD Brooklyn feel in South Williamsburg. We live above the restaurant.

WHEN I WAS back in Japan, my dad took me took a restaurant by the ocean that served sea urchin and squid over rice with egg yolk in the center. It's the best thing ever.

I WANT to eat that before I die.

» FATHER FRED MARANO «

PRIEST

I WANTED to be a priest starting when I was 11. I'm what they call womb-to-tomb.

MY PARISH is in Gravesend, Brooklyn—Saints Simon and Jude.

WE HAVE a lot of older Italians who attend mass, but we also have young Mexican families coming in to our services. And there are a handful of Chinese.

WE WANT TO put up a banner in front of the church to welcome people in four languages.

MY FATHER worked at Pier 4 in the Brooklyn Navy Yard. He went there every morning for almost 30 years.

THE MOB approached him many times. He respectfully declined.

TRAGEDIES HAVE always been a struggle for me.

IF I KNOW the family well, I'll go see them right away and not say anything. I will just hold their hands.

PEOPLE WILL SAY that the 1950s were the golden age of American Catholicism. [In Brooklyn] there were 8-10 masses filled per week.

EVERYONE STRUGGLES with doubt.

FAITH AND CALLING comes from the Lord.

MY FAVORITE MASS is Holy Thursday. Because that's the one where we remember when Jesus washed the feet of the apostles to show humility.

I LIKE TO keep it simple. Short, ten minutes at the most.

I MAKE A constant effort to be relevant and pique their interest.

A FEW WEEKS ago I discussed *50 Shades of Grey*. And I used to listen to Z100. I would say, "Has anyone heard the song, "In Da Club"?

⫸ JO FIRESTONE ⫷

COMEDIAN

TO LIVE IN Brooklyn, there are sacrifices that have to be made.

ALL OF THE sewage from the whole block backed up into our apartment. Also I think there's a spider infestation.

IT'S THE BEST apartment I've ever lived in—apart from the poop and the spiders.

I THINK THE funniest moments are the most unexpected ones.

WHEN I THINK about bad things that happen and find humor in it, it feels like I have more control.

I GET A LOT of material from being dumped.

MY MOM IS the funniest person in our family, only she doesn't know it.

YOU THINK THAT something will be funny and you try it out.

IT'S THE CHAOS. That's the whole thrill.

WHEN IT WORKS, when the audience is jumping on every word, when you can barely get them out fast enough, when they seem to cherish them in a way only laughter can show — it feels pretty awesome.

THE WORLD'S TINIEST Comedy Club was an installation I did in Manhattan with dolls and miniature stuff. People could come in and do their standup.

THERE ARE LOTS of people in New York who are down for weird shit.

IT TAKES A certain amount of presence to laugh. You have to really be there before you can let loose.

I USUALLY JUST have a kernel of an idea and I flesh it out with the audience. I want to get on stage as soon as possible.

IF YOU LET an idea sit too long you start to have doubts and that's poison.

⫸ KERRY DIAMOND ⫷

FOOD EDITOR AND RESTAURATEUR

THE FIRST big moment for the restaurant was when the first person walked through the door.

YOU WORK HARD, hope to get press, but you think, "Will we have customers?"

ONE OF OUR early customers got engaged, got married, had a child. And we saw all of those major moments. That's what makes it so rewarding.

BROOKLYN HAD a terrible reputation when I was growing up in Staten Island. It was a place you lived if you didn't have a choice.

TEN YEARS AGO, I went to a birthday party in Carroll Gardens. I fell in love with the neighborhood.

A FEW DAYS LATER I put a contract on my apartment.

WE WERE EXHAUSTED and broke from Seersucker. But everyone thought Smith Canteen was meant to be. It's been our anchor.

CALLS ABOUT doing a cookbook turned into thoughts about an annual magazine. And, *Cherry Bombe* began.

WOMEN IN THE food industry are not represented in media the same way men are.

CHERRY BOMBE snowballed and peopled wanted to write for it and it coincided with a new wave of feminism. Women wanted their voices to be heard.

IT'S SUCH A formidable group. It brings me to tears to see all those women in one magazine.

WALKING IS huge. Sometimes I'll walk home from our office in Manhattan. It's when I get some of my best ideas.

BALANCE? I'm slightly bored with that conversation, since I don't have any in my life.

INSTEAD, I'M TRYING to simplify life when I can. And I'm trying to live in the moment. That's balance for me.

⟫ SAM ZYGMUNTOWICZ ⟪

LUTHIER

EVERY VIOLIN I make is destined for someone.

START TO FINISH, one takes about six months.

I READ A BOOK about a violin-maker when I was 13 and just got captivated.

I CAME TO Brooklyn in 1980 right out of violin making school. My brother lived in Park Slope and I slept on his floor.

WHEN YOU'RE making an instrument, you're making it for a specific purpose, and you can judge whether it's good or not. It's not subject to whim like the world of fine art.

I DON'T TALK about cost.

I'M ALWAYS sourcing wood. It's kind of like having a wine cellar.

TOPS ARE MADE of spruce. Of the European woods, it's the lightest per unit of weight. Makes it very resonant. Backs and sides and necks are maple.

I LEARNED FROM a French teacher there's proper use of the knife, a lot of body mechanics in it. You learn how to control force, apply it with great control and delicacy.

YOU CAN'T BELIEVE that something this light can fill an entire concert hall with sound.

YOU HAVE TO feel the authority of your teacher. Not because they're your boss, but because they're a master.

I WAS ASKED by Isaac Stern to copy his Guarneri. At the time, Stern was the king. It was very intimidating to simultaneously work for one of the great musicians of all time and reproduce one of the greatest violins in history.

BUT WE LIVE in the same physical universe, we use the same materials. If it was doable by them it's doable by me.

THERE'S NOTHING so good that it can't be better.

»» REUBEN REUEL ««

FASHION DESIGNER

AS A KID, I was always picking out my mom's and my sister's clothes. People always knew me as the stylish one in the family.

WHEN I LOST my job in 2012, I just said, "Ok, I cannot work for somebody else anymore."

I BOUGHT SOME fabrics, made some styles, put it on Etsy, and it just hit.

THE WHOLE FIRST year of Demestiks, I was living in Midwood and I was working in my bedroom all day long. That grind helped me understand that making clothing was really want I wanted to do.

BEYONCÉ WORE my clothes and posted on Instagram. When that happened, people were like "Oh my God!" but I just wanted to be at home, chillin', working.

I STRIVE FOR quiet success.

I DO THINK the Beyoncé thing put me in a place where people saw me as a real designer.

MY PROUDEST moment? Being able to live solely off of Demestiks. Not going back to a nine to five. Being able to live freely.

LIVING IN New York for me is about freedom.

I GET UP at nine, get myself together, eat breakfast. Around 11, we start cutting fabric, doing the orders for the week. It's all pretty normal. I'm not over-thinking anything.

I GET INSPIRATION from passing people on the street.

MY FAVORITE Brooklyn season is fall. The layers, the coats and wools and all that. I love seeing how people mix it up.

WE SELL THROUGH Etsy all over the world. London. Paris. China. Just the other day I saw someone post my clothing from Australia. It's amazing to see.

SOMETIMES I CAN'T believe that this is my life.

⫸ JOSEPH VOLPICELLI ⫷

BARBER

I CAME HERE in 1956 from Italy, and I came to work in Park Slope in 1961 and here we are. Still.

THE ITALIAN, it's always there. Nobody could take that away. Nobody!

NO! I NEVER lived in Park Slope. I lived in Bensonhurst until 1982, and then in Manhattan Beach for 33 years!

I WAS 16, and we took a ship to America, the Andrea Doria. Two months after our trip, the Andrea Doria sank near Cape Cod. It was like we'd lost a family member.

PARK SLOPE back then, you would see signs on the cars saying "Please don't break the glass, there's nothing in the car."

YOU COULD BUY a brownstone for $30,000.

NOW THESE NEW people from all over the country, they hear Park Slope, Park Slope, Park Slope. Boom.

ALL OF A SUDDEN Brooklyn is a brand!

THERE'S NOT REALLY anything to miss other than the people. Unfortunately, they're gone to live somewhere else or they're gone [points up to the sky].

THE LADY IN the first chair, Charmaine, she's been here 30 years. Lana's been here 19 years. Alex was a young kid when he first came, now he has six boys. Susan's here 11 years.

IN THE MID-70S, when everybody with the long hair, business was very bad. Nobody around here was getting a haircut.

MY GRANDDAUGHTER, the younger one, she calls me Nono.

"NONO, MY BANGS are getting too long!" she says.

WHO OTHER THAN a doctor touches your head the first time that you meet the person?

⫸ CHRISTIE CHOW ⫷

SCHOOL DIRECTOR OF OPERATIONS

WE HAVE 90 seats in our fifth grade class. Over 600 families applied this year.

EVERY MORNING, we greet every student at the door. When they walk through the threshold of the school, they are ready.

I BLOCK AND tackle. That's my job.

A KID throws up. A parent calls with a question. A bus breaks down. We take away distractions and pain points, so that our teachers can teach.

IT'S AMAZING WHAT a surprise lunch can do for teacher morale.

I LIVED IN Hell's Kitchen when I started, so to get to work, my wakeup was 3:45am. That's one reason why I moved to Brooklyn.

CURRENTLY WE HAVE 313 students. Ninety-eight percent black and two percent Latino. Eight out of ten qualify for free or reduced lunch.

WE NAME OUR classroom groups after alma maters.

HARVARD, SPELMAN, Fordham, Vanderbilt. From day one, graduating from college is the goal.

A SAFE ENVIRONMENT does so much for creating real, even unlikely friendships.

STRUCTURE LETS for a kid to be a kid. Leave them alone and kids can get lost in the shuffle.

GIRLS CAN WEAR a tie also, but only if it's done right. It can't just be a fashion statement.

OUR SEVENTH GRADERS read *The House on Mango Street*. Eighth graders are reading *Animal Farm*.

THE DIFFERENCE between good and exceptional is using data. We're constantly looking at what's working best.

GOING HOME AT 7pm feels early.

⇛ EDWIDGE DANTICAT ⇚

WRITER

IN HAITI, whenever someone said they were going to the United States, they would say they were going to New York.

MY IDEA of Brooklyn though, was of the cold place where my parents lived.

WE SPOKE TO our parents every Sunday from a phone booth in downtown Port-au-Prince and tried to catch them up on our lives.

I CAME TO New York when I was 12. It was a great shock. I remember looking down from the airplane and seeing New York City below. It was so huge and full of lights.

I'M GOING to have so much to do here, I thought.

IN MY childhood mind, I imagined that my life would be touched by each and every one of those lights.

WHEN I WALKED down the hallway in our building in East Flatbush, every door was closed. I remember being struck by that. Why would they keep their door locked? What were they afraid of?

MOST OF the people were Haitian, or from some other part of the Caribbean.

THE FIRST BOOK I ever owned was Ludwig Bemelmans' *Madeline*. My uncle gave it to me. I remember holding that book in my hand and thinking, This is what I want to do.

I WANTED TO tell a story that people didn't have to speak aloud, a story that they could hold in their hands.

MY FATHER was what was then called a gypsy cab driver. I got to see a lot of Brooklyn that way.

AN AIRPORT TRIP was a gold mine.

AFTER MY first novel, *Breath, Eyes, Memory*, was selected for Oprah Winfrey's book club, my dad told me, "Well, now you

have enough money for medical school."

....

WHEN I FIRST saw my parents' tax return, as I was applying for college, I was shocked. How had they raised four children on that, I wondered?

MY PARENTS are both gone now. But it was their courage and sacrifice that made possible the lives we now live. I owe everything to the trip they took to Brooklyn.

....

IT WAS A leap of faith.

ESSAYS

Stories about a beloved neighborhood bookstore, surprises in Green-Wood Cemetery and a look-back at the riots of 1977. Plus, a poem from Walt Whitman.

⋙ THE PARAKEET ⋘

Written by **MARIE-HELENE BERTINO** | **ONCE UPON A TIME** a cargo ship unloading in the Brooklyn Navy Yard dropped a crate that cracked in two and exploded into thousands of green and lemon parakeets. Some built homes in the spires of Brooklyn College. Some nested in the mausoleums of Green-Wood cemetery, enjoying its startling views of the harbor and The Statue of Liberty.

Absolutely no one in Green-Wood cemetery is trying to be anything they're not. They're dead—no talking them out of it. This is one of the reasons I decided to run its periphery after years of running Prospect Park. The park had begun to depress me. Having only three months of good weather translates into enormous pressure to be outside when it's warm—using nature as your treadmill, hurling plastic objects across the meadow, spreading an artisan cheese across a roll. One day the activities seemed dishonest, the people under duress, not letting on how maybe they'd rather be inside with the shades drawn, staring off.

Green-Wood cemetery has a more acceptable ratio of truth to beauty. Its perimeter is 3.5 miles and its flora is abundant and fragrant. Even when I'm running through one of the more disparate sections, when it's just me, sidewalk trash and a few braked Big Rigs whose drivers are conked out in naps, the smell of lilac emanates from inside the gates. Trash and lilac is a dynamic that makes sense to me.

The parakeets are resourceful, accidental immigrants. They roost in utility pole transformers that warm them during Brooklyn's frigid winters, causing innumerable problems for Con Edison. Their stick nests are complicated interconnected series of apartments with separate entrances and garages. Hard to relocate.

I see the parakeets when I run. Arcing out over the hills, or perched in trees overlooking mourners, fanned amidst the branches like a colorful firework.

I live in a Brooklyn neighborhood called Windsor Terrace that is bordered by Green-Wood cemetery on the west, Prospect Park on the east. The folks who live here have nicknamed it "Old Brooklyn" because many of them have owned their homes for over fifty years. Fifty years is considered a long time in America. I moved to the neighborhood to have a quiet place to write my speculative fiction stories.

Sound had been the major feature of my previous neighborhood in Queens. My apartment had been situated under the elevated 7 train, next to the Long Island railroad, and beneath the flight patterns of two international airports. Every ten minutes the Express train shook the wine glasses in our cabinet. A Halal meat cart company's headquarters was in our basement. They'd haul their heavy carts past our bedroom window precisely at 6:30 a.m. every morning.

Our wine glasses, our bedroom window. Which had become my glasses, my bedroom window. During the aftermath of a seminal break -up, untrue friends shuddered away from me like bones shed meat in boiling water. My life had become the sound of metal scraping against unrelenting concrete. I began to feel like a photocopy of myself.

When a friend was leaving her apartment on East 4th Street in Windsor Terrace, she asked if I'd like to take over the lease. I packed my wine glasses and my two cats, and I moved.

In April of 1912, in a French village so scant it does not qualify for maps, my great-grandmother fell in love with a gypsy boy and became pregnant. Concerned she would disgrace the family, her father banished her, buying her a third-class ticket on a ship that was sailing for America. My great-grandmother was 18 years old. Her name was Jeanne. Her father's name was Baptiste. The village's name was Gazave, and it was built into the foothills of the Pyrenees Mountains. I don't know what the gypsy boy's name was. The ship would leave from Cherbourg, France on April 10th, and take 15 days to scoot across the Atlantic Ocean before arriving at Ellis Island in New York.

The backyards of East 4th Street butt up against the backyards of East 3rd Street. From my second floor window, I can see no fewer than ten of them. Some yards are meticulously organized into what is plant life and what is a table and chairs. Some, like ours, are overtaken by evergreen trees. All of the yards comprise a busy avenue for animals crossing from either the park to the cemetery or vice versa. I imagine a bird gathering twigs in the park, then flying over our yards to its cemetery pad. A raccoon with an elegant suitcase. A squirrel hoisting a hobo bag over its shoulder. It is a dangerous journey due to the dogs of Brooklyn, tied and watchful in our backyards, who have been known to thrash a possum or stray cat.

When I was growing up, my family had several dogs and cats but the first pet that was solely mine was a green and yellow parakeet I named Micky after my favorite member of The Monkees. Micky was mine to feed and groom and clean and maintain, a prospect that, at nine years old, I was too young to be terrified by.

Micky and I spent many happy afternoons together. I would read and he'd sit on his perch and sing or make the gravelly, garbled sound I considered a secret between us. I read every parakeet book I could find and memorized several facts. Parakeets have a third eyelid. Parakeets have monocular vision, which means they use each eye independently. They can turn their heads 180 degrees because they have more neck vertebrae than humans.

I loved Micky, even though he figure-eighted away whenever I tried to pet his velvet, avocado-colored forehead, which is called a crown eye.

One day, I decided Micky was a vegetarian, like my Mom. I replaced the seeds in his feeding dish with chopped up carrots and lettuce. He didn't seem to like them but I knew with time he'd get used to it. Days went by, then weeks. I assumed he would eat when he got hungry enough. I didn't notice when he stopped singing. I found him at the bottom of the cage, stiff and heavy. The first time I'd ever seen something dead.

After that I mistrusted myself as a caretaker. I never again wanted to be the only thing standing between a living thing and death.

Something happened that changed their minds.

Maybe the gypsy was begging to see Jeanne, or she him, or perhaps Baptiste realized they couldn't wait that long to ship my great-grandmother away from France. For whatever reason, Jeanne needed to get gone sooner. So Baptiste bought another ticket for a different ship that would leave on April 4th, six days before the original ship. They took the train to Le Havre and my grandmother boarded the S.S. Niagara on April 4th, 1912. Did she have morning sickness? Did she look back as she crossed the gangway or did she stare stubbornly forward? I don't know any of these things.

I know she was at sea for eleven days. I know that on April 10th, the day she had originally planned to leave, the S.S. Niagara hit ice off the coast of Newfoundland. The collision dented the bow plates and the ship began to leak. The crew set off an S.O.S. signal, which at the time was a relatively new way of asking for help. A nearby ship rushed to aid, but the S.S. Niagara crew was able to repair the damage themselves. Everything went back to normal. The ship continued on.

Four days later, the ship my great-grandmother was supposed to take, the RMS Titanic, would hit the same ice off the coast of Newfoundland. The captain would be rendered paralyzed by indecision, the life boats would be lowered without being even half filled, and the ship would sink with most of its third-class passengers trapped below deck.

Imagine the relocations that spiraled out of that mistake.

Windsor Terrace's local shelter has a constantly evolving menagerie of animals found on the street or surrendered by unwilling or incapable owners or pulled from their wild lives in Prospect Park. The shelter and its supply store are run by a man named Sean Casey. He rarely speaks to me even though I'm there several times a week, carrying teetering stacks of cans to the checkout, or asking if any dogs need walking. He is a neighborhood celebrity who has rehabilitated and found homes for countless animals, infiltrated fighting rings and freed all the dogs chained to the walls. His exploits are documented on the shelter's blog.

One week Sean camped out on the Brooklyn railroad, tracking a pair of wild pit bulls that had been attacking local dogs. The pit bulls lived in a hovel no one could find and had outsmarted several teams from the SPCA. Sean spent a week living and thinking like the wild dogs, until one night he caught the duo's male member. The bitch continued to elude him. Every night she'd bay and howl, heartbroken and calling for her mate.

The neighborhood felt a surprising amount pity for this hurt creature that almost overrode the horror we felt for the dogs she had attacked. Every day we checked the blog to see if she had been caught. One day a picture was posted of Sean standing next to a chocolate colored pit bull who seemed too puny to be causing such ruckus.

That's when we realized we had hoped she'd stay free forever. Or at least I had.

Speculative fiction is sometimes called fabulism, lumped under the umbrella term of magic realism. There are as many different ways of defining it as there are writers and readers. In a classical magic realist story, the dead walk freely among the living and flying things can symbolize the transition a character makes from one social class to another, from one world to the next, or from the land of the living to the land of the dead. An indicator that you are within the realm of speculative fiction is that something happens that does not obey the laws of physics. It is not unusual for someone to turn into a bird or a butterfly.

A few years ago, I went to the animal shelter to buy cat food. Bending to reach a particular can, I noticed a dainty cage under a pile of empty crates. I peered inside and found a tiny dog with enormous ears, sitting politely on a spread of newspaper. His quivering brown eyes reminded me of my grandmother's and he looked like a miniature fox. Sean told me he was a Papillon who had just been surrendered. His owner was moving to an apartment that didn't allow animals. So here he was, shivering in a cage.

Papillon, I said. The French word for butterfly.

My apartment, a one bedroom with two cats and no washer and dryer, was not suitable for a dog. However, I adopted him, for two reasons. The first was that I thought my grandmother had sent him to me. The second was that I missed her and having a family so much it had become an ache I had to pull aside to do everyday things like errands, the way you pull aside a curtain to enter the bath.

I imagine my great-grandmother on that enormous ship staring out of a porthole and panicking. Then I pluck her off the S.S. Niagara and place her onto the lower decks of the Titanic where she would have been locked behind partitions along with the other non-English speaking third-class passengers. In addition to social reasons, this was so the immigrants could access Ellis Island from a different entrance where they could be questioned and documented. Fewer than half of the third class women on the Titanic survived. It is likely that Jeanne would have perished, along with my grandmother who was growing inside of her.

SHE HAD ALWAYS FELT DIFFERENT THAN THE REST OF HER FAMILY. THIS EXPLAINED WHY.

But they didn't perish. When the S.S. Niagara delivered my great-grandmother safely to Ellis Island on April 15th, 1912, the clerk asked her two questions. They were the same two questions they asked every immigrant because someone official had decided that useful things could be gleaned about a large swath of people by how they answered them.

Can you read?

Can you write?

Her answers are recorded on the ship's manifest.

Yes.

Yes.

Jeanne traveled to the boarding house where other people from Gazave had settled. There she met the gypsy's brother, Pierre, the white sheep of the family. They married. It was the early 1900s, when people still had secrets and the world was small enough for coincidences. That October Jeanne gave birth to my grandmother, and Pierre raised his brother's daughter as his own.

When my grandmother was sixty-five years old, Jeanne told her that the man she thought was her father was actually her uncle. Her father was the gypsy, not the white sheep. My grandmother said this revelation was and was not a surprise. She had always felt different from the rest of her family. This explained why.

Relocating is traumatic. It can cause a dog to be abandoned in a cage. It can lead to a studio apartment with possums in the backyard, a running habit. It can maroon exotic birds in a land with an unfriendly climate.

Last week a parakeet sat in a patch of grass inside the Green-Wood cemetery gate, watching me as I went running by. I slowed and halted in front of it. It side-eyed me with interest.

Hello, bird, I said.

It did not answer but allowed me to admire it. The smart tufts of lime green feathers like a hat, its regal nape and mantle. Parakeets are twitchy, afraid of what's above and behind them. Obsessive-compulsive, they perform every movement several times.

Are you enjoying the winter?

It shrugged and shrugged and shrugged. *I like the quiet.*

Does it make you feel isolated?

Whenever I want I can fly to Coney Island, to the Cloisters, to Queens. I can see all the way to Mexico.

But don't you get lonely?

I am far from alone, it said, blinking and blinking and blinking.

I looked up and the trees were filled with birds. Red-throated, blue-billed, speckled-tailed something-or-others. An array of parakeets blinked amidst the branches like a yellow and green constellation.

I live between a park and a cemetery, but which is which might surprise you. Every October the park dies, while the cemetery teems with life.

Parakeets have anxiety but they are not afraid of death. They sleep inside of death. They nuzzle between the shoulder blades of a stone angel, in the corners of crypts, or the cracked-out shelf of a mausoleum.

Parakeets do not engage in debates about social media on social media. They do not reveal their political views and think most people are overrated. They have ambivalent feelings about the term "unofficial mascot of Brooklyn College." They have soft underbellies and have lost almost all of their Spanish, which is a shame, but gets filed under *things we shed to belong.*

Certainly we can assume there are nights when they're homesick for Argentina. When they fly to the top of the highest spire at Green-Wood cemetery and gaze at the ships criss-crossing the harbor.

I'm not from Brooklyn, either. Like the parakeets, my great-grandmother and, it figures, I, are here because someone made a mistake. Like the parakeets, my people are nomadic and nervous. But I stay and stay and stay, even when the cold feels like nails scraping against my DNA echo. I walk my dog. I run the same terrain over and over to get strong. When I feel lonely, I drive to Valentino pier and watch the ships. I'm no longer scared to be the only thing between a living creature and death. My husband says this is because I'm more maternal than I allow myself to believe. I mother everything, he says. Him, our animals, our friends, strangers, ideas of things. I feather our nest in Brooklyn's unfriendly winters so we stay warm. I keep a cheerful color. I am a parakeet.

MARIE-HELENE BERTINO'S debut novel, *2 A.M. at The Cat's Pajamas,* was named an NPR Best Book of 2014. Bertino won the Iowa Short Fiction Award for her story collection, *Safe as Houses.* She has also written for *The Millions, The Wall Street Journal* and *The Huffington Post.*

»» SHELFTALKER ««

Written by **EMMA STRAUB**

The staff at BOOKCOURT is both good-looking and well-read, the books are well displayed, and the children's section is appropriately in its own little nook, perfect for whiling away the hours. Singles say the store is excellent for date browsing as well.

I WROTE THAT BLURB for *The Village Voice*'s Best of New York issue in 2005, four years before I started working at the bookstore. It's a little bit like calling my older self good-looking [thank you, younger self], but more than that, I feel like it's proof that the store and I were always meant to be. When I wrote the blurb, I lived a few blocks away, having just moved in with my then-boyfriend [now husband], and we would often amble the aisles before or after dinner in Cobble Hill. I meant every word, except for the date browsing, which I'd completely made up, based on the fact that the owner's young son Zack [younger than me by a few years, then in his early twenties] was a gorgeous flirt with dark hair and bright blue eyes, and every heterosexual woman I knew in the neighborhood wanted to sleep with him.

BookCourt opened in 1981, when Henry Zook and Mary Gannett were just a couple of kids, both only twenty-seven years old. I love to think about what they were like then—the high rounds of her cheeks, his broad shoulders—and wonder what they imagined the future might hold for them and their little store. It's so easy to look at the neighborhood and to see the bookstore—spacious, light, crowded with well-dressed starlets—as a given, but it certainly wasn't. Is there any greater piece of advice in New York City retail than to buy the building? Henry and Mary bought the building.

The store takes up two storefronts on Court Street, in what is now prime Cobble Hill retail territory—there is a Rag and Bone shop across the street, the kind of clothing store with low lighting and one leather jacket hanging in the window, and a James Perse expensive t-shirt store down the block. A Barney's Co-op—the only one in Brooklyn—is around the corner. A couple of years ago, there was great consternation at the bookstore when it was revealed that J.Crew was planning to take over the deli on the corner where the staff often ran to buy mid-shift bottles of water and Gummi Bears. Thankfully, the Gummi Bears remain in place, at least for now.

When I was in high school, about ten blocks away from the store's front door, the neighborhood was full of old Italian ladies making mozzarella and Middle Eastern spice shops along Atlantic Avenue. When my male friends would walk through late at night, they worried about boys with baseball bats, a threat that always seemed like something out of a previous century, or maybe a movie musical. I never went to BookCourt as a teenager—I commuted to Brooklyn from Manhattan's Upper West Side, and I never stayed in Brooklyn after school unless I was going to a friend's house. Even if I had visited, it wouldn't have been the same shop that exists now—for the first fifteen years of its life, BookCourt occupied a single storefront with a basement, which I would guess maxed out at about seven hundred square feet. In 1996, when I was a sophomore in high school, Henry and Mary bought the building next door, and expanded the store into the space that had previously been a flower shop, which added another four hundred square feet or so. That was the

ANYONE WHO CHOOSES TO WORK THE FRONT LINES OF A SHOP SELLING BOOKS IS GOING TO BE BOTH CHATTY AND A LITTLE BIT INSANE.

incarnation of the store that I wrote about for the *Village Voice*, cozy and densely packed. In 2008, they built a giant addition onto the back of the flower shop space—the Greenhouse, they called it, because the room was where a greenhouse for the flower shop had once stood—tripling their square footage. A Barnes & Noble had recently opened a few blocks down Court Street. BookCourt was doubling down—they knew what people in the neighborhood wanted—a beautiful space filled with a curated selection of books. Places to sit. No coffee, no wifi. It was a middle finger to the idea of the corporate giant—they were staying put, and getting bigger. The Greenhouse was [and remains] studded with skylights, with a high ceiling, and walking into it feels like a magic wormhole straight to California.

I started working at BookCourt in 2009, just after I returned home to New York City after graduate school. I knew Zack a bit, and we'd been in touch about setting up an event I was doing at the store for a small book of mine, a single short story that was charitably being published by a small press as a novella. I was looking for a job—any job—on Craigslist, and there it was, a posting for a bookseller gig at BookCourt. I wrote to Zack immediately, and we scheduled an 'interview,' which is a very loose word indeed for what transpired. I met Zack at the benches in front of the store's red door, and we went down the stairs at the center of the paperback fiction room, and then we sat down with his father, Henry, also a handsome flirt, who was wearing his running clothes. I would soon learn that Henry was usually wearing his running clothes. [For sartorial fairness, I should add that Mary is most often found in a sky-blue cardigan that matches her eyes, which are even brighter and prettier than her son's.]

I had my book party for the little novella on a Sunday night, and started working at 9am the next day. My book—all twenty-seven pages of it—was that week's number 1 fiction bestseller. No one on the staff could have cared less. Everyone wanted to talk about Roberto Bolano's early work, or John Williams's *Stoner*, or Barry Hannah's *Airships*, or, even more so, who else on staff they wanted to sleep with. I fell in love with the job immediately, the way some people feel about cocaine or SoulCycle. How had I survived so long without this particular pleasure?

Any long-standing retail establishment that sells culture is going to be staffed by a motley crew of opinionated weirdos, and BookCourt is no exception. The staff is big—maybe fifteen people, almost all of whom work part-time, for less money than I now pay my teenage babysitter. In my time, there were always a solid number of recent college grads in cute outfits, the boys with short, tight pants, and the girls in enormous sweaters and mini-dresses that made shelving books a potential peep-show. About two-thirds of the staff were Ph.D students, writers and poets. The rest of the staff were eccentrics, gray-haired and intermittently surly, sometimes in Hawiiaan shirts. Anyone who chooses to work the front lines of a shop selling books is

going to be both chatty and at least a little bit insane.

We arrived in waves—Chad, Adam, Brisa, Molly, me, Andrew, Maryam. Jack came back after some years away. Glenn, a Brit. Lauren became the new Molly. Christien became the new Chad. Laura and Martha got fired for no reason. Stephen couldn't have been fired if he set the building on fire. Steve, my favorite employee, came to BookCourt from the funeral parlor down the block, where he also did odd jobs. He packed up the cardboard boxes and wore an FDNY fleece and protested for years when the store cat went to live with Henry after befouling a stroller or two. Nothing was fair or equal. We were lopsided in our talents. Zack handsold the same few books to anyone who asked [Arthur Bradford's *Dogwalker* and Thomas McCarthy's *The Remainder*, or a Michel Houellebecq], but I had fallback favorites too [Meg Wolitzer's *The Wife*, Elaine Dundy's *The Dud Avocado*, Donna Tartt's *The Secret History*.] We wrote ecstatic shelftalkers, the little blurbs written by booksellers in our Staff Favorites section, and we rejoiced when someone took our advice and forked over cash for our beloved sentences and paragraphs.

Working for a family business is almost irresistible—among the staff there were usually half a dozen writers, and we would all joke about it—which one of us would write the sitcom, the short story, the novel inspired by the store's owners, and the rest of us, all of us with our own hilarious storylines. Henry and Mary had split up some years before [I would rather die than ask for more specific details], but continue to run the business together. They get along remarkably well—no worse than any married couple I have ever seen or interacted with in a prolonged way, with no more than an errant eye roll. I know a thousand nominally happy couples who I regularly see fight far more often and awkwardly. Still, one would occasionally get asked to do something [shelve these books here!] and then asked to do the direct opposite thing [shelve them over there!] by different family members. Staff members spent a lot of time pretending to stare at the ceiling and/or the floor. Zack, a talented photographer, has since moved to the Virgin Islands, where he does lots of things that don't involve working with his parents. We all understand.

In my tenure as a bookseller, I hid behind the counter twice. The first was when Jennifer Egan came in shortly before the publication of *A Visit from the Goon Squad*, and I was too full of love for her to speak. I ducked behind the counter and waited until she was gone to come out. The second time was when a boy I'd hooked up with in high school in particularly gross circumstances [a friend's pullout sofa, very bad oral sex] came in and browsed—the fact that the store was so close to my school was both a boon and a police baton to the knees. On the one hand, it meant that I could handsell copies of my short story collection, published in 2009 by a very, very small press, to every single person I knew. Parents of friends, former teachers, everyone— the print run was 2000, and I sold 800 of them over the counter at BookCourt. On the other hand, it meant that I often had to make small talk with people I had never liked, such as my friend's stepfather who accused me of stealing something from him in 1995. I didn't.

There were other writers who charmed us all—the drinkers and the story-tellers, the nervous, the Irish. One former staff member who was always on drugs walked in on Jonathan Lethem in the bathroom. There were the writers who knew how boring readings could be and instead played Donna Summer on their iPads and did stand-up comedy instead [Colson Whitehead], and the writers who did the old-fashioned boring reading thing so well that we all wept from the beauty [Colm Tóibín.] Someone passed out when Don Delillo read, which I assume was because it was too hot and crowded, and not because of the material. Jonathan Franzen endeared himself to me hugely by hurrying to Paula Fox's side at his packed event for *Freedom*—he was clearly so honored and moved to have her there, and made sure she was comfortable. Yes, Jonathan, we all thought, yes, you can stay. [Another favorite to handsell: Paula Fox's *Desperate Characters*.]

Of course, in a beautiful, clean, safe Brooklyn neighborhood, most people are more interested in movie stars than writers, even the booksellers. It's humiliating, the ways in which a bookseller will attempt to have a conversation with a browsing movie star. *I love your yoga mat*, Hope Davis. *Sure is rainy out there*, Paul Giamatti. *I love your overalls*, Emily Mortimer. Paul Dano and Zoe Kazan were our little ringers, our favorites—they bought books all the time. Most of the famous customers were the ones you would assume you would like in real life, whose noses were a little bit funny to be proper leading ladies, who looked like they had messy piles of books on their nightstand. The bad movie stars were the ones who came in with their friends and tried [loudly] to tell them everything that they'd ever read—we loved those the most, because we got to make fun of them the moment they left. I once had to ask poor Natalie Portman for her billing zip code because our credit card machine wasn't functioning properly and she looked at me as if I'd asked for her home address and social security number.

I quit when I was three months pregnant. It was January, post-retail Christmas rush. Anyone who works retail, whether it's books or broomsticks, will tell you what Christmas is like, a zippy blur. Wrapping presents, enormous stacks of books. People will buy whatever you tell them to, so desperate to buy anything. *I need something for my step-grandfather, I need something for a tween, help!* [*David McCullough, Rainbow Rowell.*] I was down to two shifts a week, and loath to give it up, but my double deadlines were looming—my baby was due in August and my new book was due in September. I was about to go to Mallorca to do research, and it seemed silly to not just quit. I met Mary in her apartment [she lives above the store, of course] to tell her, both about quitting and the reason why, and we both cried.

I'm still in the store every few weeks—my son, now a year and half old, loves to pull books off the shelves, and will sit and read as I saw thousands of other tiny people sit and read in my tenure. On a recent visit, my son and I were sitting on a sofa in the Greenhouse, reading. A young man—maybe twenty-three years old, in a cardigan and glasses—was working his second shift. He ducked behind the counter to ask his co-worker how to do something—ah, the keystrokes I've forgotten. I welcomed him to the store, as if it were my place to do so. I didn't tell him that I was a writer, or my name. I just said, "I used to work here. It's nice, isn't it?" He nodded, flustered, wanting to get it all right. He might last six months. He might last six years. I hope the store lasts forever.

EMMA STRAUB is a New York City native, and is the author of the short story collection *Other People We Married* and the novels *Laura Lamont's Life in Pictures* and the *New York Times* bestseller *The Vacationers*. Her writing has appeared in *Vogue, Elle, New York, Lucky, The Wall Street Journal,* among others. She lives in Prospect-Lefferts Gardens, Brooklyn.

HERE COMES
THE NEIGHBORHOOD

Written by **MICHAEL DALY AND DENIS HAMILL**

Originally published by *The Village Voice* on July 13, 1977

The following Village Voice *cover story about the 1977 New
York City blackout taps into complex issues of race, economic
disparity and police brutality, equally relevant then and now in
Brooklyn. In retrospect, that summer's crippling financial crisis,
the Son of Sam murders and a scorching heat wave proved
to be a terribly perfect storm. So, when the city lost power for
two days that July, looting, vandalism, arson and hundreds
of violent episodes [many involving law enforcement] became
emblematic of a troubling era in the borough's history.*

The lights have been out for five minutes.

The people on Brooklyn's Broadway are going shopping.

Nineteen-year-old Jamar Jackson takes his second slug of
pineapple soda as he watches his friend Bobby Stamps put his fist
through the plate-glass window of Al-Bert's Men's Wear. Stamps reaches
his bleeding hand past the shattered glass and grabs two shirts. An empty
bottle of Wild Irish Rose crashes through another window. Now comes
a brick. Hands are everywhere, stripping mannequins, grabbing shirts.

Jackson's heart is pounding. He snatches a pair of brown corduroy
pants. He realizes how easy it is. A gun barks. Jamar runs onto the
sidewalk and bumps into a man holding a .32 caliber automatic over
head. The man squeezes off five more shots. The muzzle flash lights up
a gang of kids pulling on the grate covering the next store.

"They're hittin' Busches's Jewelry," somebody screams. More
glass shatters. Jamar hears a stampede racing toward him in the
darkness. Bodies press against him and carry him down the street.

Edwin Velez's television has been dead for 10 minutes. His girlfriend screams at him for not paying the Con Ed bill. Jumping off his tattered sofa, Edwin leans out his window. The entire neighborhood is dark. He hears glass breaking on Broadway, a half-block up Gates Avenue.

Edwin races into the hallway on the top floor of the four-story walk up. Neighbors are pushing and shouting in the stifling darkness.

"They're goin' in the stores," a woman yells. Edwin is knocked halfway down a flight of stairs by a sweat-soaked, 300-pound woman.

"Get out of my fuckin' way," the woman bellows as she tramples Edwin. "I'm goin' to get me something before the greedy niggers take it all." Edwin drags his 10-year-old cousin, Cesar, from the building's vestibule. On Gates Avenue, the stampede toward Broadway is on.

"Come on, man," Edwin tells Cesar. "It's a riot."

"That's when they come in a shoot you," Cesar says, pulling back into the vestibule.

"No, it's when you take what you want form the stores," Edwin says.

From the west, thousands pour out of a 630-acre slum called Bushwick. The area was first settled by the Dutch West India Company in 1660. The first blacks in Bushwick were slaves on the Dutch tobacco plantations. The Germans replaced the Dutch and were, in turn, squeezed out by the Irish. Then came the Poles and the Italians.

Today, there are no Dutch, Germans, Irish, Poles, or Italians. Today there are 225,000 blacks and Puerto Ricans living in 42,000 dwelling units. One quarter of these units have been classified by the City Planning Commission as "badly deteriorated." Bushwick High School, originally designed for an enrollment of 2000, has 3000 students. An average of 400 drop out each year.

From the east, thousands converge on Broadway from Bedford Stuyvesant.

Until 1940, Bed-Stuy was a middle-class enclave. But Harlem was bursting with immigrants from the south. Drawn by jobs at the Brooklyn Navy Yard and inspired by Duke Ellington's hit, "Take the A Train," an avalanche of poor blacks poured into Bed-Stuy via subway. After 25 years of blockbusting and redlining, Bed-Stuy was declared "the heart of the largest ghetto in America" by the Housing and Urban Development Administration.

On both sides of Broadway, unemployment hovers around 80 per cent. Half the families live on less than $4000 a year. Forty per cent are on welfare. The infant mortality rate is the highest in the city. In 1967 the City Planning Commission reported that the area "...urgently needs almost any type of community facility and service——housing, schools, health services, parks, supervised recreational activities, language classes, low-interest loans for home-owners and businesses, social services, cultural activities, libraries, more job opportunities and learning programs, and improved sanitation and police protection. Assistance must be provided quickly."

It is 10 years later, and the people in Broadway are assisting themselves. Edwin and Cesar dash up to Broadway.

Four men wrench a parking meter out of the concrete and batter the door of a jewelry store. On the third blow, the door blasts open. A crowd gathers. Edwin and Cesar are pushed into the store. A man with a baseball bat attacks the display cases. Broken glass sprays through the flashlight beams. A shard slices Edwin's cheek. Holding his shirttail to his face, Edwin feels-around the dark floor. He finds two watch cases and slips them into his pocket.

> **"I'M GLAD THEY'RE DOING THIS," HARRY SAID, AS THE MOB CARTED OUT THE SHOE BOX'S INVENTORY.**

The incoming tide of looters pushes Edwin and Cesar further into the store. It is pitch black and the heat is suffocating. Somebody has a transistor radio.

"There's a party atmosphere in Manhattan," a WINS newscaster says on the radio. Police sirens drown out the radio and probing beams of red light cut through the darkness. The tide turns and Edwin is carried toward the front of the store.

"God, don't shoot," a woman screams. Edwin steps on a leg as he scrambles for the exit. One cop beats a steady, sharp tattoo on the sidewalk with his riot stick. The other cops simply watch the looters flee. On Gates Avenue, Edwin, breathing hard, opens the watch cases. They are empty.

"Shit, man," Edwin says. "All that for nothing. I was scared in there. My heart was doing a heavy tango."

Twelve-year-old Harry Brown stands outside the Everready Furniture Store. He is holding two notebooks he has just swiped from a stationary store. Across the street, a mob storms the Shoe Box. A year ago, Harry went into the Shoe Box to buy a pair of Pro-Keds. The shoes cost $12.82. Harry has $12.80.

"You don't get the shoes 'till you have the full amount," the white storekeeper had told Harry.

"I'm glad they're doing this," Harry said Wednesday night as the mob carted out the Shoe Box's inventory.

By now, Bobby Stamps has 200 pairs of dungarees, seven leather jackets, and dozens of shirts, all from Al-Bert's Men's Store. Nothing is left in the clothes store. Stamps races a stolen panel truck down Broadway from a luxury-item store called Time Credit.

A sign behind the accordion grade reads: COME IN. YOUR CREDIT IS GOOD WITH US. Bobby wraps a chain around the gates and hooks it to his truck's bumper. He pops the clutch and the truck jumps forward 30 feet. The accordion gates follow. Bobby heaves a garbage pail through the plate-glass window. Sixteen minutes later, he has five color television sets, two air conditioners, and a rack of wristwatches piled into his truck. Bobby stops to help an elderly man load a sofa onto the roof of a station wagon and races home.

"Plug them in and see if they work," Bobby's mother says as her son carts in the booty. Of course, there is no electricity.

Against all of this, Captain James Wynne of the 81st Precinct has only 22 men at his command. The station house's emergency generator kicks in moments after the lights go out. The first reports of looting come 10 minutes later. The dispatcher shouts that, along with the phones, the main radios are dead. The hand-sets will only receive.

Wynne orders the men in the station house into patrol cars and barks one simple command: "Shoot the looters."

Wynne is in the lead car when the first cops hit Broadway. He and three other cops jump out in front of Time Credit. One last looter brushes past Wynne with a vacuum cleaner. The mob has moves up Broadway to another store. Wynne follows.

"We must have been outnumbered 70, maybe 80-to-1," a cop from the 81st Precinct says later. "And that was after reinforcements were brought in. I don't know how the hell nobody got killed. It must have been the magic of the blue."

The luxury items disappear into the tenements. Now, the shoe stores topple. Sneakers and high-heeled shoes litter the avenue. A young black kid races past two white cops with a paper bag full of shoes.

"Look, there goes a shoe-shine," one of the cops says. The other cop laughs. Youths swarm into the bike shops and ride away on the inventory. In the gloom, someone offers a $200 Peugeot 10-speed for $40. Duos zip from store to store on Mopeds, one kids driving, the other holding the swag.

A young black kid named Maurice Stone stands on the avenue with a new shirt, new jeans, and new sneakers.

"I wish I could get me some bikes," Stone says. "I been in a lot of stores, but I mostly got clothes. Most of the bikes is gone. I got a watch, but it don't work I don't think, so maybe I'm gonna sell it. "

The cops start to make the first collars. Two cops tackle a six-foot black man as he comes out of J. Michael's furniture store and drag him to a patrol car. Another cop grabs a teenager by her hair and pulls her toward the same car.

Two television sets, 11 pairs of Puma sneakers, and a sofa richer, the 28-year-old Walter Bean ambles through the front window of the corner Key Food. Bean starts filling a shopping cart with meat.

"Fuck the whole thing," a tall man at the back of the store shouts. A match flares, but goes out. Another one sputters but also goes out.

"Anybody got any matches?" the tall man shouts. A middle-aged Puerto Rican woman stumbles back into the darkness. She hands matches to the tall man, but they drop to the floor. The tall man and Puerto Rican woman are now down on their knees searching for matches. The tall man finds them and kicks more papers into a pile he's already made against a back wall. The fire spreads and the smoke is soon rolling across the ceiling and curling up the side of the three-story building.

"Burn, baby, burn," the arsonist shouts, silhouetted against the orange glow of the flames. It isn't until the next day that anybody realizes 100 local part-and full-time jobs have also "burned, baby, burned."

Walter Bean escapes, pushing a shopping cart laden with chicken fryers, bacon, and ground chuck. The chicken fryers are marked at $1.08 a pound. The bacon is tagged at $1.60 a pound. The ground chuck is going for $1.49. At Sloan's on Sheridan Square in the West Village, the fryers go for 89 cents a pound, bacon for $1.35 a pound, and ground chuck for $1.39 a pound. Tonight, for the first time. Key Food is underselling Sloan's.

Fire trucks scream out of the Engine Company's 222's station on Reid Street. By 4 a.m. there are fires raging on Broadway. There are not

enough firemen to handle them. They head first for the buildings where people live. The El running above the avenue traps smoke and blacks the moonlight. The only light is from the shooting flames.

As the engines pour water into the blaze in Key Food, Dean Zule, 22, is in an alleyway on Green Street starting a barbecue. A neighbor brings down a can of lighter fluid and an armload of steaks. Zule turns the steaks with a screwdriver his brother stole from a hardware store. He raises his right hand, which is covered with a grimy, blood-stained bandage.

"The new sign is the fist with a towel wrapped around it," Zule says. "That's the power salute. This time it was flashlights, not guns. All power to the looters. Shit, I cut myself because I didn't have no towel."

Zule spits a steak with a screwdriver, gnaws on the suet, and breaks into a big, greasy grin. The sun is rising over Bushwick.

THURSDAY, JULY 14

Slats of sun lance through the tracks of the rusting El. Shards of plate glass glisten in the street. Debris is strewn along the sidewalks and gutters. Yawning policemen loiter on street corners, watching black children dressed in short pants and new sneakers scavenge in the litter. A dog with mange tears at a sooty steak in front of Key Food. A police helicopter cuts through the smoke that billows up from the burning buildings. Along a 34-block stretch, from Myrtle to Stone Street, store after store has been ripped open. Gates have been wrested from their runners. Cellar boards have been pried loose from their concrete foundations. Most of the saloons, liquor stores, fast-food joints, and storefront churches have not been touched.

Thousands of people are still in the streets. Music blares from new tape decks and transistor radios. Batteries are going for two dollars apiece. One man dances a soft shoe with a mannequin. More cops in riot gear troop onto the avenue. In small knots, people mutter that many of the cops are not wearing badges or nameplates. This, people say, is the first sign that the beatings and shootings are about to begin. One cop from the 83rd Precinct, badge number 15101, is asked why he wears no nameplate.

"Because we lost them," he answers. Another cop, standing in front of the Reid Avenue station house, brandishes a table leg as a weapon.

"I don't fucking feel like wearing no badge," he says. A heavyset cop, badge number 29065, races toward a dozen kids who are trying to match odd sneakers. His baton cracks a shin bone and the kids scatter.

His nameplate is covered by a black elastic band.

Six kids sit on a rooftop, their legs dangling four stories above a team of firemen fighting a store blaze. A stream of water hits a 20-foot bed of embers. Dense smoke drives away the kids.

Twenty-seven fires are burning on Broadway. Great streams of water pour into the street from the fire sites, forming large black ponds at the blocked-up sewers. One exhausted fireman named Tommy O'Rourke stands shin-deep in a pond of pater. A mannequin's arm floats next to O'Rourke's legs. He gulps from a glass of ice water. Black mucous runs from his nose. His teeth are creviced with soot. His eyes are bloodshot. When he spits, his phlegm is black.

It's a motherfucker," O'Rourke gasps. "When you're fighting a fire, been up all night, maybe 18 hours now, and you know the prick that lit this job is across the street laughing at you and probably torching another joint."

As the afternoon deepens, thousands more crown onto the avenue. The power is back on. A J train thunders overhead. The looters cheer and then invade Vim's shoe store near Linden Boulevard. One woman sits on a burned-out car and measures her foot with a shoe-size ruler. A wedge of police move in on the store. Most of the looters flee. Some stay and exchange taunts with the police. Most of the cops edge away, their hands on their sidearms, their nervous eyes checking the rooftops for snipers. One cop rushes forward and clubs a Puerto Rican man with a bat. The other police pull the cop away from a fast-growing crowd.

"These motherfucking cops are pounding us," the Puerto Rican man says. "They ask no questions and they just beat your motherfucking head. They want static, motherfucker, they get static."

A black man with blood seeping from under his hair walks to the front door of the 81st precinct.

"I want to talk to your boss," the man tells a cop stationed at the door. "One of your boys hit me upside my head just because I was carrying a pipe."

"What were you carrying a pipe for?" the cop asks.

"Shit man," the complainant says. "Just 'cause you carry a pipe doesn't mean you're gonna use it."

Then the power dies again. The stoplights are out. Tires screech.

Horns blare. Police sirens wail. Shouting matches break out. The sound of breaking glass picks up.

A squad of Savage Skulls appears, flying their war colors, carrying longer sticks than the cops.

"God is giving the poor people their bread today," a gang member named Smokey says. "The poor people only want the same things the cops have. TVs, nice furniture, shit like that. And food. People have to eat. The cops are lucky they don't want blood. But before this is over there might be some blood anyway."

"The cops started this shit, man." Blue Eyes, the supreme president of the 14th Regiment of the Bushwick Division of the Savage Skulls, says. "They're taking things off looters, my people, and putting it in their cars and takin' it home to their houses, man. One cop broke a little girl's hip. The cops are handling it all wrong, They beating up black and Puerto Rican people. The cops should be in the stores. If there was a cop in a store, nobody is gonna go in there and risk getting killed for a pair of sneakers." Blue Eyes points across the street. Two cops in riot gear are guarding a burned-out Key Food. A hundred yards down the street, people are leaving a grocery store with six-packs of warm beer.

> **"I'M SCARED. IT'S THE APOCALYPSE OUT THERE. IF THIS GETS WORSE, I'M MOVING BACK TO BARBADOS."**

"I went to some of the precincts," Blue Eyes says. "I told some of the brass there that they doin' it wrong. I know some of the brass. I been on TV shows with 'em. You know what they told me? They told me to kiss their ass. Well, if that's what they want, we'll handle this shit. We had 82 guys here this morning. I'm thinkin' of calling in all the gangs and handling this thing right. We have a right to protect our community against police brutality and shit. We might finish this thing off completely, man, tonight."

And now, the night is here and there are no lights. Bands of youth rove the avenue toting two-foot flashlights, baseball bats, iron pipes, two-by-fours, and even hammers. The police wander aimlessly up and down the street. Every 20 minutes a caravan of eight patrol cars crawls down Broadway. The looting pauses as the cars pass, then continues. People talk in low tones. There is too much tension to shout.

Seventy-five looters have been arrested and packed into the pens at the Reid Street station. In the booking room, stolen goods are piled head high.

"What do they expect us to do with all this shit?" one cop asks another.

"Who the fuck cares?" the other answers. "We'll just shovel it into barrels and send it down to the Property Clerk's office. Let them figure it out. The entire garage outside is already filled. This is just the overflow."

A third cop is in the rear of the precinct, taking inventory. After 24 hours on the street, he was ordered back to the station, and handed a clipboard and a stack of forms.

"Where the fuck is that other Quasar TV?" he says to another cop.

"How the fuck should I know?" the second cop says. "I only dealt with Zeniths."

"I feel like a fucking stock boy," says the first.

"A stock boy with a gun," says the second.

"Fuck you," says the cop with clipboard. "Now where is that other Quasar?" He is asked how many television sets were brought in. He answers, turning into a salesman. "You interested in a floor model or a portable?" Turning back into a cop, he says, "I honestly don't know. I have one here, a Quasar, I can't even find. It might be buried under that mountain of shit."

He points to the mountain of shit. It includes: paper towels, frozen pizzas, baby clothes, Kotex, Pampers, jackets, lounge chairs, mattresses, couches, lawn mowers, vacuum cleaners, dishes, silverware, and hundreds of other items.

A detective walks up to the cop.

"I heard you need a hand," the detective says, offering the cop a mannequin's hand.

Over at the desk, a sergeant points to a porcelain statue of Stan Laurel.

"Can you imagine going to jail for stealing that?" the sergeant asks. "This is another fine mess Stan Laurel has gotten somebody into."

At the other end of the room, a half-dozen civilians huddle on plastic chairs. They've come to the precinct for safety.

"I'm spending the night right here," one of the civilians, Teddy Eve says. "I'm scared. It's the apocalypse out there. If this gets worse, I'm moving back to Barbados. There's no money in Barbados, but they don't have the apocalypse down there."

"I was terrified something would happen to me." A West Indian woman sitting on the next chair says. "It's horrible, just horrible. It's all been destroyed." A minister from Bed-Stuy stands in the doorway. Earlier in the day, Mayor Beame had put out a call for all religious leaders to cruise their neighborhoods to "restore the calm."

"I went out there," the minister says. "But they all too busy stealin'."

The power comes on at 9:30. Thirty-seven officers sit in the muster room, waiting for the next caravan run. Black cops stay in tight knots. They only join white cops at 9:50, when it's time for another sweep. Donning helmets and swinging sticks, the cops jump into the row of squad cars.

By the time the cops hit Broadway, the crowds have moved away from the avenue's streetlights and dispersed into the dark side streets.

"There's nothing left to steal that's worth getting shot over," a middle-aged black man says as he walks down Putnam Street. "And I know that if this goes on much longer, the cops will be shooting."

Arson is now the main event. On the corner of Somers and Stone Avenue, a five-story warehouse is blazing out of control. The first alarm had come in at 5:30 p.m. By 6 it had reached 5 alarms. It is now 10:30 and the blaze is still out of control. A super-pumper has been brought in. Crowds from Broadway move in to watch the show. Seven firemen have already been injured.

The fire jumps 50 feet across the street. Three other buildings and two cars catch fire. The factory's cornice crumbles, crushing a fire chief's van.

Miguel Pérez, 20, who lives in the last remaining house on the block, watches the blaze. He claims he saw a man light the fire.

"This cop hit a tall, skinny, colored guy when he caught him looting the warehouse," Perez says. "There was stereos, TVs, clothes—that kind of stuff. So this guy gets mad because the cop hit him. He comes back later with two red gasoline cans and pours them into the building. He lit that gas up. Then he soaked some of the other buildings in gasoline." Part of the factory collapses, sending columns of sparks 100 feet into the night sky.

"I gotta make sure this guy don't torch my place, man," Perez continues. "I'm telling you, I know this guy's face. I've seen him in the neighborhood. Me and my two brothers are gonna fuck this guy up good. Maybe I'll kill him. I haven't decided yet. He had a big wide Afro. I'd like to burn it off."

Tonight is the night of the fire union election. Michael Maye has lost to Richard Vizzini. Neither of them has come out to Bushwick. So far, neither has Beame or Fire Commissioner O'Hagan. Deputy Chief Tortoriello has—since the lights went out.

"Nah, they ain't been out here," Tortoriello says. "That's the big time. This is only Brooklyn." He chuckles and returns to the fire.

FRIDAY, JULY 15

The fire burns through the night. At daybreak Michael Perez is still standing watch. He says he will not go to sleep until he is sure the arson and rampage are finished. As the warehouse continues to smolder, people start to reappear on Broadway.

"It looks like Sherman marched through here on his way to Atlanta," says one morning stroller.

Those stores that were not hit are open for business. Paul Alexander, the manager of National Shoes near Linden Boulevard explains that, although his store went untouched, business is bad.

"There has been no business today," he says. "There won't be for a long time. Everybody around here has new shoes."

Up the street, Eddy Mizihi sits in a cream-colored Plymouth outside of what was once his clothing store.

"I might open it again," Mizihi says, "If Mayor Beame gives me the money. If not...what am I going to do?"

Ahmed Muharran stands in front of his grocery at 1385 Broadway. He hasn't slept in 48 hours. From the moment of the blackout until this morning, he stood in the doorway to his shop with a double-barreled shotgun. Right now he's open for business, but he keeps a police baton in his hand.

"Look, you have to protect yourself," Ahmed says, keeping his eye on a 12-year-old standing near a potato-chip rack. "I told them when they tried comin in they were going to get hurt. They went away and robbed somebody else. Maybe tonight I'll sleep. We'll see."

Outside Ahmed's store, Rodney Washington and Wallace H. Jones are discussing the situation.

"This Con Edison makes me laugh," Washington says. "They blaming the whole goddamned thing on some act of God. Now how can they say that when Con Edison is God?"

"I don't give a damn who's to blame," says Jones. "What I want to know is where the fuck was the Civil Defense? The Civil Defense is supposed to help to police. I know because me, Wallace H. Jones of 710 Bushwick Avenue, was in the Civil Defense for 11 years. The Civil Defense is supposed to be here when the bomb drop. Well the bomb done dropped."

Jones, who became a building contractor after he retired from the Civil Defense, walks into Al-Bert's Men's Wear next door to Ahmed's grocery store.

"You need some repair work in here?" Jones asks Maurice Phillips, the owner of Al-Bert's. Phillips looks around the store. The windows are smashed. The bare shelves are splintered.

"Maybe," says Phillips, laughing. Phillips first came into the store 11 years ago to but a pair of pants on layaway plan. A salesman told Phillips that the store needed a stock boy. Four the next four years, Phillips stacked shirts and pants for $95 a week, an exceptional wage for black workers on Broadway. In 1970, Phillips took out a Small Business Administration loan and bought out the white owners of the shop. Phillips started to experience what he calls the "pitfalls for black businessmen." Factories sent him inferior merchandise and refused to give refunds on damaged clothing. In 1974, Phillips grossed $274,000, but not a single bank would extend him a loan. Two years ago, the store's basement flooded, destroying $70,000 worth of clothing. According to Phillips, the landlord, Broadway Realty, Inc., refused to accept responsibility for the damage and shortly thereafter, raised the rent. Phillips was hit with a spate of break-ins and hired the Holmes Protection Agency to watch his store. For $387 a month, Holmes promised to call Phillips the moment the burglar alarm went off. Last year, Holmes twice let the alarm ring for more than nine hours. Phillips was cleaned out both times. At the same time, the Chemical Bank was sitting on a $15,000 installment of Phillips's second $60,000 SBA loan.

"You're a turkey," an officer at Chemical recently told Phillips. "You're headed for bankruptcy. We've been telling you that for a year."

"Then why aren't I bankrupt?" Phillips asked. "You refuse to give me any working capital and I'm still in business."

"I was looted before the riot," Phillips says. "The people were looted, too. You have to look at the total economic conditions, the frame of mind of the people. I'm more angry at Chemical Bank than I am at the people. Window shopper finally got a chance to fulfill their desires and not just live with the bare necessities. Everybody stepped into the television commercials for a few hours and took what they wanted."

As Phillips talks, the mayor and an entourage drive past the store in two air-conditioned buses. When the buses stop farther up the block, the mayor and 50 reporters and cameramen exit onto Broadway. Fire engines are parked at crazy angles along the streets. Smoke still wafts from some of the ruins. A hydrant is still gushing on the corner. The stream of water runs swiftly along the curb, carrying assorted debris— cancelled checks, price tags, pages from ledgers, mail orders, the scribbled paperwork of small businesses. Beame, with the help of an aide, hops over the stream and starts talking to newsmen.

"Jobs, jobs, jobs, how about some jobs," a group of black kids on the other side of the street chant.

"He's here to discuss foreign aid," one reporter jokes. Exactly 11,360 feet of news film is shot of the mayor as he walks through the devastation. The mayor directs an aide to expedite emergency housing to a woman burned out of her apartment. The woman kisses the mayor's hand.

"What's all this?" a black youth asks a friend.

"They making a commercial," the friend answers.

Mayoral candidate Bella Abzug is also in the area. At the 81st Precinct, she examines the loot piled in the building's garage. Dressed in a sporty summer dress, Abzug says she still stands behind the right of policemen and firemen to strike.

"What if they went on strike during something like this?" she is asked.

"They wouldn't," she answers.

"What would you do if you were the mayor?"

"Mobilize the community organizations and get them into the street."

After Abzug leaves, Gary Jenkins, a local resident says: "The community was mobilized. They were all out lootin'." Jenkins grabs a shopping cart and pushes it down the street.

"Going shopping?" Jenkins is asked.

"No," Jenkins says, "I already been."

Ron Shiffman, director of the Pratt Institute's urban planning center, is also in the neighborhood.

"This whole thing about giving out Small Business Administration loans to merchants who lost their businesses is a sham," Shiffman says. "There isn't the structure for giving out the loans. The mayor is playing politics with people's lives. It's an ugly thing to see all this looting, for sure. But the people who live in Bed-Stuy and Bushwick have had their lives looted for years."

Shiffman comes from the Bud-Stuy tradition inspired by Robert Kennedy in the early 1960s. Speaking at a community meeting in Bed-Stuy in 1966, Kennedy talked about the future that arrived on Wednesday:

"If this community can become an avenue of opportunity then others will take heart…but if this community fails, then others will falter and the noble dream of equality and dignity will fall with it."

As night falls on Broadway, only the people who live here every day remain.

Bobby Stamps is hawking $36 French-cut jeans on a street corner for $8 a pair. Jamar Jackson is with him, wearing a gold Aries necklace. Jackson is an Aquarius.

"I wish there would be a blackout every night," Stamps says. "Shit, I'd be a millionaire."

On the roofs of the Bushwick housing projects off Fulton Street, a huge clearance sale is under way. Hundreds of tenants examine piles of televisions, stereos, appliances, and shotguns. A 15 year old is handing out complimentary cassettes with each tape recorder. Most of the merchandise is going for less than 10 per cent of retail value.

Along the avenue, the bars are doing their usual business. Music and drunks float out of Beulah's Goodtimers, the Utopian Lounge, and Jukes Lounge. A transit cop is ticketing a battered Chevy parked at a bus stop. Groups of Puerto Ricans sit around card tables on milk boxes and play dominoes. Salsa blares from a new tape deck. The stores along Broadway are either shuttered or gutted. There is already graffiti on some of the plywood covering the broken windows. On yellow spray paint, someone has written "DETROIT".

Blue Eyes and Smokey of the Savage Skulls stroll down the street.

"I'm glad it cooled out last night," Blue Eyes says. "The police kept cool and it worked out. It's better that way. Maybe the cops will try to understand the street people."

Inside the 81st Precinct, Captain Wynne is ready to go home. He looks exhausted, but agrees to answer some questions.

"Did you expect the looting?" he is asked.

"You expect what you get," Wynne says. "But I'm not surprised."

"Do you expect any more trouble?"

"Not if we keep the lights on."

"Why weren't the cops wearing badges and nameplates?"

"I wasn't looking at cops."

"Have there been any arrests for violent crimes in the past three days?"

"No."

Behind Wynne, there is a bulletin board with a dozen pictures pinned to it. WANTED FOR MURDER, a sign above the picture reads. Last year, there were 23 murders, 50 reported rapes, and 1100 armed robberies in the 81st Precinct.

"It was a bitch," a desk sergeant says after Wynne leave. "But at least nobody got hurt bad. You'll see the violence start up again, though. Now that the party's over, it'll get back to the nitty gritty. We'll have a stiff by morning. " The sergeant goes back to his bacon, lettuce, and tomato sandwich.

DENIS HAMILL currently writes for *New York Daily News*. He won the prestigious Meyer Berger Award for best New York City reporting. He has written for *New York Magazine*, the *Los Angeles Herald Examiner* and *New York Newsday*.

MICHAEL DALY is a correspondent with *Newsweek* and *The Daily Beast*. He was previously a columnist with the *New York Daily News* and a staff writer with *New York* Magazine. He was a finalist for the Pulitzer Prize for commentary in 2002 for his columns on 9/11.

CROSSING BROOKLYN FERRY

Written by **WALT WHITMAN**

1

Flood-tide below me! I see you face to face!
Clouds of the west—sun there half an hour high—I see
you also face to face.

Crowds of men and women attired in the usual costumes,
        how curious you are to me!
On the ferry-boats the hundreds and hundreds that
        cross, returning home, are more curious to me than
        you suppose,
And you that shall cross from shore to shore years hence
        are more to me, and more in my meditations, than
        you might suppose.

2

The impalpable sustenance of me from all things at all
        hours of the day,
The simple, compact, well-join'd scheme, myself
        disintegrated, every one disintegrated yet part of the
        scheme,
The similitudes of the past and those of the future,
The glories strung like beads on my smallest sights and
        hearings, on the walk in the street and the passage
        over the river,

The current rushing so swiftly and swimming with me
     far away,
The others that are to follow me, the ties between me and
     them,
The certainty of others, the life, love, sight, hearing of
     others.
Others will enter the gates of the ferry and cross from
     shore to shore,
Others will watch the run of the flood-tide,
Others will see the shipping of Manhattan north and
     west, and the heights of Brooklyn to the south and
     east,
Others will see the islands large and small;
Fifty years hence, others will see them as they cross, the
     sun half an hour high,
A hundred years hence, or ever so many hundred years
     hence, others will see them,
Will enjoy the sunset, the pouring-in of the flood-tide, the
     falling-back to the sea of the ebb-tide.

3
It avails not, time nor place—distance avails not,
I am with you, you men and women of a generation, or
     ever so many generations hence,
Just as you feel when you look on the river and sky, so I
     felt,
Just as any of you is one of a living crowd, I was one of a
     crowd,
Just as you are refresh'd by the gladness of the river and
     the bright flow, I was refresh'd,
Just as you stand and lean on the rail, yet hurry with the
     swift current, I stood yet was hurried,
Just as you look on the numberless masts of ships and the
     thick-stemm'd pipes of steamboats, I look'd.

I too many and many a time cross'd the river of old,
Watched the Twelfth-month sea-gulls, saw them high in

the air floating with motionless wings, oscillating
their bodies,
Saw how the glistening yellow lit up parts of their bodies
and left the rest in strong shadow,
Saw the slow-wheeling circles and the gradual edging
toward the south,
Saw the reflection of the summer sky in the water,
Had my eyes dazzled by the shimmering track of beams,
Look'd at the fine centrifugal spokes of light round the
shape of my head in the sunlit water,
Look'd on the haze on the hills southward and south-
westward,
Look'd on the vapor as it flew in fleeces tinged with violet,
Look'd toward the lower bay to notice the vessels arriving,
Saw their approach, saw aboard those that were near me,
Saw the white sails of schooners and sloops, saw the ships
at anchor,
The sailors at work in the rigging or out astride the spars,
The round masts, the swinging motion of the hulls, the
slender serpentine pennants,
The large and small steamers in motion, the pilots in
their pilot-houses,
The white wake left by the passage, the quick tremulous
whirl of the wheels,
The flags of all nations, the falling of them at sunset,
The scallop-edged waves in the twilight, the ladled cups,
the frolicsome crests and glistening,
The stretch afar growing dimmer and dimmer, the gray
walls of the granite storehouses by the docks,
On the river the shadowy group, the big steam-tug closely
flank'd on each side by the barges, the hay-boat, the
belated lighter,
On the neighboring shore the fires from the foundry
chimneys burning high and glaringly into the night,
Casting their flicker of black contrasted with wild red and
yellow light over the tops of houses, and down into
the clefts of streets.

4

These and all else were to me the same as they are to you,
I loved well those cities, loved well the stately and rapid
    river,
The men and women I saw were all near to me,
Others the same—others who look back on me because I
    look'd forward to them,
[The time will come, though I stop here to-day and
    to-night.]

5

What is it then between us?
What is the count of the scores or hundreds of years
    between us?

Whatever it is, it avails not—distance avails not, and
    place avails not,
I too lived, Brooklyn of ample hills was mine,
I too walk'd the streets of Manhattan island, and bathed
    in the waters around it,
I too felt the curious abrupt questionings stir within me,
In the day among crowds of people sometimes they came
    upon me,
In my walks home late at night or as I lay in my bed they
    came upon me,
I too had been struck from the float forever held in
    solution,
I too had receiv'd identity by my body,
That I was I knew was of my body, and what I should be I
    knew I should be of my body.

6

It is not upon you alone the dark patches fall,
The dark threw its patches down upon me also,
The best I had done seem'd to me blank and suspicious,
My great thoughts as I supposed them, were they not in
     reality meagre?
Nor is it you alone who know what it is to be evil,
I am he who knew what it was to be evil,
I too knitted the old knot of contrariety,
Blabb'd, blush'd, resented, lied, stole, grudg'd,
Had guile, anger, lust, hot wishes I dared not speak,
Was wayward, vain, greedy, shallow, sly, cowardly,
     malignant,
The wolf, the snake, the hog, not wanting in me,
The cheating look, the frivolous word, the adulterous
     wish, not wanting,
Refusals, hates, postponements, meanness, laziness,
     none of these wanting,
Was one with the rest, the days and haps of the rest,
Was call'd by my nighest name by clear loud voices of
     young men as they saw me approaching or passing,
Felt their arms on my neck as I stood, or the negligent
     leaning of their flesh against me as I sat,
Saw many I loved in the street or ferry-boat or public
     assembly, yet never told them a word,
Lived the same life with the rest, the same old laughing,
     gnawing, sleeping,

Play'd the part that still looks back on the actor or actress,
The same old role, the role that is what we make it, as
     great as we like,
Or as small as we like, or both great and small.

7

Closer yet I approach you,
What thought you have of me now, I had as much of
      you—I laid in my stores in advance,
I consider'd long and seriously of you before you were born.

Who was to know what should come home to me?
Who knows but I am enjoying this?
Who knows, for all the distance, but I am as good as
      looking at you now, for all you cannot see me?

8

Ah, what can ever be more stately and admirable to me
      than mast-hemm'd Manhattan?
River and sunset and scallop-edg'd waves of flood-tide?
The sea-gulls oscillating their bodies, the hay-boat in the
      twilight, and the belated lighter?

What gods can exceed these that clasp me by the hand,
      and with voices I love call me promptly and loudly
      by my nighest name as I approach?
What is more subtle than this which ties me to the
      woman or man that looks in my face?
Which fuses me into you now, and pours my meaning
      into you?

We understand then do we not?
What I promis'd without mentioning it, have you not
      accepted?
What the study could not teach—what the preaching
      could not accomplish is accomplish'd, is it not?

9

Flow on, river! flow with the flood-tide, and ebb with the
        ebb-tide!

Frolic on, crested and scallop-edg'd waves!

Gorgeous clouds of the sunset! drench with your
        splendor me, or the men and women generations
        after me!

Cross from shore to shore, countless crowds of
        passengers!

Stand up, tall masts of Mannahatta! stand up, beautiful
        hills of Brooklyn!

Throb, baffled and curious brain! throw out questions
        and answers!

Suspend here and everywhere, eternal float of solution!

Gaze, loving and thirsting eyes, in the house or street or
        public assembly!

Sound out, voices of young men! loudly and musically
        call me by my nighest name!

Live, old life! play the part that looks back on the actor
        or actress!

Play the old role, the role that is great or small according
        as one makes it!

Consider, you who peruse me, whether I may not in
        unknown ways be looking upon you;

Be firm, rail over the river, to support those who lean idly,
        yet haste with the hasting current;

Fly on, sea-birds! fly sideways, or wheel in large circles
        high in the air;

Receive the summer sky, you water, and faithfully hold it
        till all downcast eyes have time to take it from you!

Diverge, fine spokes of light, from the shape of my head,
        or any one's head, in the sunlit water!

Come on, ships from the lower bay! pass up or down,
        white-sail'd schooners, sloops, lighters!

Flaunt away, flags of all nations! be duly lower'd at sunset!

Burn high your fires, foundry chimneys! cast black
        shadows at nightfall! cast red and yellow light over
        the tops of the houses!

Appearances, now or henceforth, indicate what you are,
You necessary film, continue to envelop the soul,
About my body for me, and your body for you, be hung
    out divinest aromas,
Thrive, cities—bring your freight, bring your shows,
    ample and sufficient rivers,
Expand, being than which none else is perhaps more
    spiritual,
Keep your places, objects than which none else is more
    lasting.

You have waited, you always wait, you dumb, beautiful
    ministers,
We receive you with free sense at last, and are insatiate
    henceforward,
Not you any more shall be able to foil us, or withhold
    yourselves from us,
We use you, and do not cast you aside—we plant you
    permanently within us,
We fathom you not—we love you—there is perfection in
    you also,
You furnish your parts toward eternity,
Great or small, you furnish your parts toward the soul.

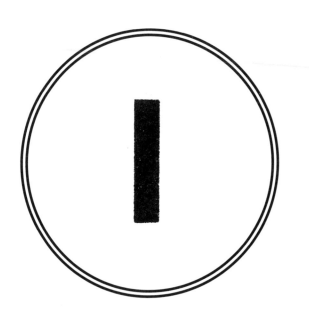

INDEX